C000047661

Contents

We Sang It Our Way

For nearly forty years, Reginald Frary has been entertaining readers with his humorous stories about singing in church choirs.

In real life, he has been a member of his parish choir for more than fifty years. He lives in Richmond, Surrey.

We Sang It Our Way

Confessions from a choir vestry

Reginald Frary

CANTERBURY
PRESS
Norwich

First published in 2001 by Canterbury Press Norwich
(a publishing imprint of Hymns Ancient & Modern Limited
a registered charity)
St Mary's Works, St Mary's Plain,
Norwich, Norfolk, NR3 3BH

Second impression

British Library Cataloguing in Publication data

A catalogue record of this book is available
from the British Library

ISBN 1-85311-432-4

Typeset by Rowland Phototypesetting Limited,
Bury St Edmunds, Suffolk
Printed and bound in Great Britain by
Bookmarque, Croydon, Surrey

Preface

How did I become so enmeshed in all this church choir business? What a game of chance life is when one small incident, one brief remark, can decide the direction of a lifetime!

From earliest childhood I was taken by my parents each Sunday to choral evensong at Sir George Gilbert Scott's grand, fashionable church of St Mathias on Richmond Hill, with its very splendid choir. During my first years, there was a church-warden who was one of those authoritarian figures who, by common consent, take charge and rule. He ruled on the town council. He ruled at the church. He was a Scot, a distinguished hydraulics engineer, a short, sturdy, elderly man with boundless energy and determination.

One Sunday, a minute or two before evensong was due to begin, he leaned into our pew and said to my father, 'The laddie must join the choir' – just that brief command.

After the service the organist spoke to my father. 'If he is accepted as a probationer,' he explained, 'he will have to attend choral evensong on Mondays, evensong and choir practice on Tuesdays, the same on Thursdays, full practice on Fridays and we have a considerable number of choral weddings on Saturdays for which the choir is needed. And on Sundays, of course, he will be needed for all three services.'

'Yes, I understand,' said my father.

'Would he be able to manage these duties?' asked the organist.

'Yes! Oh, yes!' replied my father promptly. 'Certainly!' And so it was arranged that I should join the choir. No one had asked me anything. No one had even taken any notice of me standing there. And the next week I became a choirboy.

I've been a chorister ever since, singing at three services every Sunday, and at scores of weddings, for more than fifty years.

I am forever grateful to that old Scottish autocrat who, all those years ago, decreed 'The laddie must join the choir'.

1

Preferably a Philistine

'I hope he won't be a genius. Geniuses can be quite a nuisance.'

'Or a moron – morons can be awkward, too.'

'Or a relative of the vicar. Fancy having another one like him.'

'Or a philistine.'

'I don't know about a philistine. Perhaps a philistine would be best for us. You know how the vicar likes to call us philistines because we're always singing old favourites and won't do anything new.'

'Yes, I reckon you're right. Let's look out for a philistine.'

The discussion was taking place among members of a West-Country parish church choir in the vestry after Sunday evensong. As a not infrequent visitor in the choir and an old friend of one or two of the senior members, I was a privileged eavesdropper.

Things were getting unusually exciting for the choir in those days. A new organist and choirmaster was in the process of being chosen – the previous one having decided that his destiny lay in playing tea-time piano music on a cruiseliner – and a short-list of three applicants had been agreed upon. The idea was that each should be allotted a weekend during which he would conduct the Friday night choir practice and play at the three Sunday services, thus giving the choir the opportunity to make their choice of a leader. The first of the three was to take charge of the choir during the following weekend.

'A full house,' beamed the vicar, as he surveyed the crowded choirstalls on Friday evening. 'Splendid! Splendid! And to conduct the practice tonight I have the pleasure – indeed, very *great* pleasure – in introducing' – and he went on and on about the small, apparently multi-talented young man at his side, who kept on rising on the balls of his feet and seemed to be critically appraising the chancel ceiling. Eventually, at a loss for any more words of praise, the vicar reluctantly stopped and stepped back.

The young man stood before us and I had the most forceful feeling that he would have appreciated it if we'd all jumped to attention and saluted. We didn't, of course, and, having lowered his eyes to regard with silent distaste half a house-brick that was supporting the end of the battered choirstall at his side, he looked us over with an expression that could have been one of puzzlement or contempt or both. 'I suppose you *can* all read music?' he said, letting his eyes drift to the ceiling again. There were mumbles and grunts in reply, but no definite confirmation that some of us could read music, or admission that most of us couldn't and had to rely on the choirmaster bashing out the tune over and over again on the vestry piano until we knew it by heart.

The young man picked up a psalter. 'I don't like the pointing in this psalter,' he announced. 'I want you to sing a few verses of Psalm 67 until I can stand it no longer. Then I'll show you how to alter the pointing so that the words make some sense.'

We'd only got as far as the second verse when he stopped us with a pained expression and frantic, flapping hands. '*This* is how it should be sung,' he announced, and proceeded to sing the whole psalm through in a thin, wailing tenor that moved the vicar, standing next to me, to breathe, 'Beautiful, oh, beautiful . . .'

And for the rest of the practice the choir didn't have much to do at all except listen to the young man warble through all the canticles, psalms and hymns for the Sunday services, doubtless so that we should realize how much beauty we had missed in all the years before his arrival. The final item of the practice was the evensong anthem, which members of the choir had specially chosen. It was a regularly bawled old favourite by Barnby, and it so upset the young man that he couldn't even contemplate rehearsing it. So he replaced it with something by Tallis which no one knew, but it didn't matter because the young man was more than ready to sing the solo parts to us, which immediately restored his composure and sent the vicar into ecstasies of delight.

Needless to say, the choir didn't choose this particular genius for the post of organist and choirmaster. But neither did they later endorse the other applicants. One was an iron-faced, cynical-eyed gentleman who looked like a retired school-master of the old school, whose main aim at the practice seemed to be to make each member of the choir sing a scale solo three or four times while he made continuous little tut-tutting sounds and breathed hard. And when at last we did get the chance to sing together, he punctuated our efforts with observations such as: 'We are not putting just that little bit *extra* into it, are we?' and 'We mustn't forget what we've been told just two minutes ago, must we?'

The other applicant, a nervous, worried-looking young man, didn't seem to have his heart in the proceedings at all. Either he'd just had a row with his girlfriend, who was sitting in the front pew with a very unfriendly expression on her face, or he didn't like the sound of the organ or the vicar. He certainly didn't like the sound of the choir and seemed to be talking to himself through most of the practice. A choirgirl who was standing nearest him reckoned that he was making rude remarks about our vocal abilities. Be that as it may, he finished the practice in no time at all and was promptly marched away by the unfriendly looking girlfriend. So neither he nor the iron-faced cynic got the job and we still had no choirmaster in sight.

Some time later I was at the church again, on this occasion helping out at a Saturday wedding service for which it had proved difficult to muster an adequate choir at short notice. For weeks, in the absence of a regular organist, a series of well-meaning members of the congregation had tried their hands at the organ ('Well, I can knock out a tune on the piano – the organ is much the same as a piano, isn't it?'), but that brutish instrument stood in its dark, cobwebby corner getting more and more surly and uncooperative as it awaited someone who would really understand it and deal sympathetically with its decades-old eccentricities. Things were getting desperate, and even the vicar had expressed the view that, although he would prefer a genius for the post, he wouldn't say no to a good, reliable philistine.

Luckily no volunteer organist was needed for this wedding. The bride was supplying her own, a favourite uncle who used to play a cinema organ in the great days when cinemas were magic palaces and not like someone's living room with a screen between the window curtains. Presently he presented himself in the vestry, a beaming, rotund little man in baggy morning dress, rather self-consciously hanging on to a grey top hat. The vicar introduced him to us and we gathered round him as he went through the list of wedding music which appeared to be scribbled on the back of a bill from the local off-licence.

He poked a stubby finger at the scrawl. 'There you are, you see. She's coming in with Wagner – you know, "Here comes the bride" – and going out with Mendelssohn. None of this new-fangled stuff. And' – his finger prodding again – 'the *old* tune to this hymn and the other two. You can't beat the old and tried stuff. Some of those parsons and organists today try to slip in all kinds of odd stuff – modern rubbish. You have to watch 'em like a hawk.'

He bustled off to the organ. We remained in a circle, looking at each other, as a single exciting thought crystallized between us. Our tenor soloist voiced it. 'A philistine!' he exclaimed. 'A real philistine! Do you think he'd like a regular job?'

The wedding service went off splendidly. Everyone in the choir knew every note of the music – had known it since childhood – and they all sang merrily if not melodiously. The organ seemed to sense that it had found an understanding friend and its sound was happy.

After the service the little organist was obviously delighted with our suggestion that he should consider the post of permanent organist and choirmaster. 'Often thought I'd like to tackle a church organ,' he admitted, 'but never did anything about it. Y'see, it's the choirboys. Never married. Had no kids. Don't understand 'em. Wouldn't know how to keep the choirboys in order. Not a clue, y'see.'

Reluctantly, some of us saw him off to the wedding reception and I returned to the vestry for a

coat I'd forgotten. One of our sopranos was there putting away the music. She was a beautiful girl and wholly charming and, it transpired, had just hurled a choirboy head first through the vestry doorway into the churchyard rubbish tip. He was always referred to by his mother as 'our super little kid' and for months had enjoyed nothing better after a service than skateboarding round the vestry at breakneck speed and laughing joyously and heartwarmingly at the resulting chaos and surge of unecclesiastical language.

When some of my choir colleagues heard about the choirboy-hurling incident, they went to the vicar with a suggestion and the vicar got in touch with the philistine with the same suggestion. Now the philistine is happily installed as organist and choirmaster and he doesn't have to worry overmuch about discipline among the choirboys. He has a delightful deputy who manages that side of things very ably.

2

The Eye of the Beholder

The new vicar in the village where my old wood-work master, Hacksaw, is organist is very proud of the village church. He says it's unique and full of character and keeps on photographing it and getting artists to draw bits of it. It looks like an eighteenth-century folly. It wasn't built as a folly, of course, but throughout the eighteenth and nineteenth centuries enormously rich and generous patrons and devil-may-care local builders with widely differing artistic tastes – or no taste at all – had the time of their lives adding bits of thatching and fat stone cherubs all over the place, and knocking out peerless Norman doorways and medieval windows to accommodate an outsize memorial chapel with a music-hall ceiling and a hefty castellated west porch reminiscent of the entrance to a Victorian railway tunnel.

The new vicar's admiration knows no bounds. He likes the choir too; he reckons that never before has he come across a choir even remotely like Hacksaw's. He says they've got that elusive something that is indescribable.

On a recent fine Sunday morning when I was in the vicinity, and arrived early to sing in Hacksaw's choir, a glamorous choirgirl (Hacksaw always has glamorous choirgirls in his choir because he says that, stuck up there in the chancel in full view of everybody, the choir should at least look attractive even if they can't sing attractively) was conducting a tweed-clad, elderly, peering man with a notebook around the outside of the church and beaming at him and everything in general. I joined them.

'What *period* is the church?' asked the man, with a slightly puzzled air.

'Period?' repeated the choirgirl. 'It's all periods. We've got the lot here.' She pointed to the parapet. 'You see all those little knobs and things along the top? They were put up for Queen Victoria's Diamond Jubilee.'

'Restoration,' shuddered the peering man.

'I expect so,' continued the choirgirl. 'And this big bit stuck on the side here is a memorial chapel for the people who used to live in the big house on the green. They've all gone now, and it's a sort of borstal.'

The peering man seemed to be having difficulty in looking at the memorial chapel.

'The tower's really old,' his guide went on. 'It was here when my granddad was a boy.'

'But it's fifteenth century,' said the man.

'Yes, quite likely,' agreed the choirgirl. 'It hasn't got any electric light. The bellringers have to use oil lamps.'

'Strange!' Her charge was craning his neck sideways. 'There's a thatched roof round the back here.'

'That's our choir vestry,' said the girl. 'It used to have a tin roof, and a slice of tin fell off one Sunday evening – they say Hacksaw was going mad on the organ with a bit of Wagner (he gets out of control with Wagner sometimes, makes the whole place shake) – and this slice of tin nearly brained the churchwarden's cat so someone gave the money to thatch it – the roof, that is, not the cat,' she clarified, and her smile was irresistible.

'Extraordinary!' murmured the peering man, mesmerized. Slowly he shifted a glazed gaze to a memorial plaque on the wall. 'Late eighteenth century,' he wavered. 'Very nice.'

The choirgirl nodded at the flamboyant wording that commended the deceased. 'He used to play a viol in the gallery before we had an organ,' she explained. 'There's a lot about him in the history of the parish that my Uncle Ted wrote. You can get it for ten pence at the back of the church. The choir used to sit in the gallery in those days. I wouldn't like to do that. They had to sit on planks of wood with no backs.'

He still peered at the plaque. 'I like all those cherubs crawling round it,' said the choirgirl. 'Jolly fat, though, aren't they? If people had babies as fat as that now they'd be dead worried.'

The peering man looked up at the east window, and his voice warmed. 'Again, fifteenth century,' he almost purred. 'Beautiful fifteenth century.'

'Yes,' agreed the choirgirl. 'Funny, too. On sunny summer mornings the sun shines right on to the choir and all our faces look green and red.'

The peering man gazed at her. 'A beautiful, beautiful window. Think of it! Put here over five hundred years ago.'

'Yes,' said the choirgirl, 'and this is the vestry door. My brother – he's a carpenter – fixed it last Saturday. The old one had fallen to bits. Looks a bit new for around here, but it'll blend in better when he stains it.'

Just then the door in question opened and an agitated Hacksaw looked out. He ignored the peering man, greeted me fleetingly and urgently appealed to the choirgirl. 'I can't find the anthem copies for "Hear my prayer",' he announced.

'Where's Jack?' asked the choirgirl. 'He's got lots of places where he keeps things – oh, of course, he's on holiday.'

'I've looked everywhere,' said Hacksaw.

'Have you looked under the radiator behind the organ?' asked the choirgirl. 'There's an old shoebox – or in the broom cupboard? There's lots of junk in there.'

'The broom cupboard, ah!' Hacksaw bounced off and in a few moments was back with a wad of yellowing, tattered music. 'Good for you,' he said. 'Good old "Hear my prayer".'

'You mean we're doing it this morning?' asked the choirgirl. 'We haven't practised it.'

'Yes, we have – when we did it last time,' said Hacksaw.

'That was two years ago,' reminded the choirgirl. 'Who's singing the solo?'

'You are,' said Hacksaw. 'You'll look good singing that.'

'What about if I don't know it?' suggested the choirgirl.

'You'll *know* it,' countered Hacksaw. 'You've

14

been in the choir long enough to tackle that without much bother. We'd better just run through it quickly before people start coming into church. We can't be kicking up a row while people are having their quiet time before the service.'

'Quiet time?' repeated the choirgirl. 'They don't have a quiet time. They stand around gassing till they see the choir coming in, then they all rush for their pews. Anyway, why are we doing "Hear my prayer" in such a hurry?'

Hacksaw mentioned the name of a prominent and wealthy lady who lived in a local Victorian pile called The Towers and who was eagerly supporting the vicar's latest pet projects for the parish both financially and by the frequent loan of her grounds and luxury marquee. 'She has a sister who is visiting her unexpectedly from the States,' he explained, 'and this sister simply adores "Hear my prayer". And she's coming to matins this morning.'

'I hope we don't break down,' said the choir-girl.

'Oh, we'll manage,' assured Hacksaw comfortably. 'We always do. Look at the time we did that special request of the Hallelujah Chorus for that wedding when more than half of us were away on holiday.'

'We only had six in the choir,' remembered the choirgirl, 'and one of those had forgotten his glasses and couldn't see the music.'

'There you are, then,' said Hacksaw. 'Those wedding people were really pleased. In any case,' he concluded, 'from what I hear of the sister, she's not likely to notice any little slip-ups. She's not all that musical. She just thinks Mendelssohn is so romantic because he died young.'

Suddenly, joyously, the bells pealed forth, drowning out Hacksaw's further words.

'That's done it,' shouted the choirgirl. 'Now we can't even practise it!'

No one interfered with the doings of the bellringers because they'd been there for ever. No one really knew much about them. In fact, it was a job to tell them apart. They were all rotund of figure, wore black suits with gold watch chains and bowler hats and, when not ringing, always seemed to be keeping themselves to themselves round their own special table at the back of the bar in the Black Dog.

'We'll manage,' mouthed Hacksaw, and he beamed affectionately at the glamorous choirgirl.

And, true to form, the choir (turning up in the revered traditional manner two minutes before the service and having the anthem thrust into their hands as they scrambled into their robes) did manage the Mendelssohn very well and the glamorous choirgirl sang like an angel. After the service the sister from the States hugged her with tears in her eyes and the vicar felt sure that now, at the vaguest suggestion from him, the parish Christmas dinner and dance could he transferred from the parish hall to the ballroom of The Towers.

As I left the vestry in company with Hacksaw and the choirgirl, the peering man suddenly materialized round a corner, waving his notebook violently. 'Absolutely disgraceful!' he addressed his recent guide. 'So many awful things have been done to this church. Restoration, it's called. I call it vandalism. Look at what they did to the lovely chancel. Those awful Victorian choirstalls cluttering it up and destroying its perfect proportions. What a wicked shame. They should be swept away.'

'Swept away?' gasped the choirgirl. 'They're where the choir sit, and proportions or no proportions, we're not going back to sitting in the gallery on planks of wood with no backs.'

'Surely a small price to pay to enable your congregation to appreciate real beauty?' said the peering man.

'But the congregation couldn't *see* the choirgirls if they were stuck back in the gallery,' put in Hacksaw. And his face was a perfect picture of puzzlement.

3

A Minor Problem

I discovered the church quite by accident. I was spending a weekend in a famous cathedral city and, having finished my sightseeing earlier than anticipated, I decided to visit a nearby village with which my family once had connections.

It was on one of those delightful country bus routes where the transport company can always get you there but can never seem to arrange the timetable to bring you back. Realizing this too late, I started to return from the village on foot, and on my way stumbled on the church.

It wasn't anywhere in particular, and was hiding behind a row of sinister-looking yews. Inside the ancient porch a sad-looking notice clung desperately to a board by one bent drawing pin. 'This church is open daily . . .' it announced, and trailed off into an oblivion of weather-beaten tatters.

A great padlock held the door firmly closed, but

this didn't deter me in the least. I knew from experience that in many places it is still a time-honoured custom to welcome the visitor through the most inconspicuous and inaccessible door in the church. After a search, in which I tore my jacket on a bramble bush and turned my ankle on a weed-bedecked gravestone, I discovered a small door behind a flourishing bed of nettles. The door gave easily to my touch, and following a short sharp drop I found myself in pitch darkness on a heap of coke in the stoke hole.

As I emerged again, removing coke and a spider from my trouser turn-ups, a youthful voice announced shatteringly, 'All the runners and betting!' From behind a vault there appeared a large, round child, carrying a bundle of parish magazines. It stood watching me intently. It wore a colourless boiler suit, and its face was framed in prickly blond hair. Its sex defied identification. It said, 'My father sings in the choir.'

I never know quite what to say to children, but here I was on home ground. 'Oh good,' I replied encouragingly. 'That's nice, isn't it?'

The large round one thought about this for a moment. 'I don't know,' it answered slowly. 'My father sings with a big, loud voice and they stand him at the end of the row away from the vicar.'

'Oh,' I said, not quite so assuredly. 'I suppose he sings bass then?'

Again the child meditated, rubbing its prickly head. 'No, I don't think so,' it decided. 'I think he sings chronic. That's what the vicar says, anyway.'

Mercifully, before I had to think up a rejoinder for this, a burly young man carrying a scythe appeared from behind the chancel. The large round infant's face lighted with pride. 'That's my father,' it announced. 'He sings chronic.'

I immediately established friendly relations with Dad, who was most pleased to learn that I was a fellow-chorister. He suggested that he should show me round the church, and on releasing my hand from a vice-like, stable-scented grip, he climbed in through a window and opened the vestry door.

He took me first to see the organ which he said was a wonderful instrument, which hadn't worked for years because the pumping handle was broken and the veteran who used to operate it, dead. 'We use a harmonium,' he explained, indicating a glorious piece of Victoriana perched half on the chancel step and half on a piece of fallen masonry.

The large, round child who was by now standing on its head in the churchwarden's pew, shouted up the church, 'I'm going to be in the choir when I'm five. I shall be out of the way while Mum cooks the Sunday dinner.'

Dad glanced admiringly at his offspring. 'The kid'll make a wonderful singer,' he assured me. 'Our family is all the same.'

There seemed no answer to this, and we both continued to gaze silently at the child until it lost its balance and fell with a clatter into the aisle. Dad then stirred himself from his fond anticipations and said he was sure I would like to see the choir's large music library which had been almost entirely built up in recent years by a generous bene-factor.

We returned to the quaint little vestry. It had so much ivy growing across its latticed windows that everything looked dark green, and we could hardly see where we were going. He lighted the gas, and dragged back a curtain revealing the music library housed in two large porridge-oats boxes.

I examined a number of well-known anthems and settings and was at once struck by the fact that they all appeared to be brand new and unused. I mentioned this to him, and he gave me a look of amazement, tinged with pity. 'But we don't *do* 'em,' he said incredulously. He pointed to a small, tattered jumble of music copies on top of the piano. 'There are the ones we *do*. Why, we've sung the same anthems at all the big festivals for *years* and *years*. Our congregation likes to know what they're in for. They don't stand for all this messing about with the new stuff.'

My guide now led me into the chancel to view the choirstalls, which he said were very interesting. He was right. The book-rests and backs of the seats were a glory of amateur carving, carried out by generations of choristers who wished to perpetuate their names in that ancient place. He showed me his name, cut so deeply that a book-rest seemed to be in imminent danger of collapse. 'They do something like this at St George's Chapel, Windsor,' he informed me, 'only *there* the names are on metal plates and are Knights of the Garter or something.'

As we left the church the large, round child was stacking the missionary pamphlets neatly into a heating stove.

'Come on, Fred,' called Dad.

At last I knew! 'What a bright little boy,' I enthused.

Father regarded me, puzzled. 'Frederica's a girl,' he said.

4

The Disintegrating Choir

The choir of a nice, undistinguished, traditional parish church that I know well has a cheerful, comfortable sound that doesn't discourage the congregation from joining in the singing for fear of spoiling a perfect performance. No one is quite sure how many of the choirboys and choirgirls *can* actually sing – the choirmaster never embarrasses a chorister by asking him or her to sing a solo scale – but there is always a dependable core who know roughly what they are doing; all the children look so happy and bursting with health on festive occasions, in fact the whole choir projects such a jolly atmosphere, that it seems there is hardly a worthwhile event in the town to which the parish church choir are not invited. (They are, for instance, extremely popular in the annual horse show where they sing 'golden oldies' in the beer tent between the show-jumping events, and they collect large sums of money for charity, belting out carols in the local pubs during the Christmas season.)

Recently they have become even more important to the town, the only other local church choir being in a sad state of disintegration, thus leaving the parish church choir alone to satisfy an increasing demand on them for boisterous wedding services, jolly choral christenings and old-time music hall in the town hall.

And what of the disintegrating choir? Thrilling, wonderful things – according to their new vicar – were taking place at their church. The vicar's 'Revival and Survival' team were going in for wide-ranging rethinking and reorganization such as replacing the church's Victorian stained-glass windows with nice, light cheerful tinted glass, framing the outside notice board with red neon and uprooting the ancient font (someone has given them a 'functional' portable one) to make room for a bright, jolly coffee bar at the back of the church. Also, the vicar had decreed that the choir should cease wearing their outdated robes and come down from the choirstalls and sit among the congregation. This demonstrated that the choir and congregation were one great united family, and ensured that during the service the organist was left on his own up in the chancel and had lost all contact with the choir, whom he couldn't even see unless he leaned back at a dangerous angle and craned his neck sideways. Other notable rethinking and reorganization had resulted in the insertion of a prayer for animals at the family communion service on the first Sunday of each month – and the erection of a large notice barring dogs from the churchyard at all times (including the first Sunday in each month). These dogs included two matey hounds, an enthusiastic black and white fellow of uncertain parentage, an extremely proper Great Dane and an aristocratic poodle, all belonging to members of the choir.

So, robeless and dogless the choir were disintegrating and the parish church, in the words of their organist, was 'taking on the whole ball game'.

The greatly increased number of choral weddings being loaded on to the parish church choir meant that there was hardly a Saturday afternoon now when they were not engaged jollying along the singing on these festive occasions. They took it all in their stride, however, and didn't learn any special music, preferring to stick to the usual items they'd sung at weddings for years. So no extra practices were involved and everyone simply turned up and sang 'Praise, my soul, the King of heaven' and

'Jerusalem' at full blast. Occasionally, if the wedding couple were a little choosy musically, different music was sung – but then the participants tended to bring their own singers so the choir only had to be there and lead the bride up the aisle and look cheerful.

In my experience the average church choir rarely show much interest in the people at a wedding unless close acquaintances are involved. The choirgirls sometimes like to see what kind of gown the bride has chosen ('That's nice, I like her train and all those rosebuds round the neck'; 'It wouldn't suit you, not with that whopping great bow at the back'; 'Well, no. I'd have that a bit smaller, but it's a nice dress'; 'If you ask me, I wouldn't be seen dead in it') and there are occasional spots of high drama that the choir are in a good position to behold, such as when, too late, the mother of the bride and the mother of the bridegroom realize that they are wearing the same hats, or when the much photographed, drooled over smallest bridesmaid is sick all over her partner just as the vicar is asking the congregation if anyone knows any reason why he shouldn't marry the happy couple.

But generally the choir rip cheerfully, unconcernedly, through the whole proceedings and are out of the vestry and well away before the new husband and wife have barged their way through the crush in the church porch to pose for a few score more photos in the churchyard.

I was a visitor in the choir on a recent Saturday afternoon when we were waiting at the back of the church for the arrival of the first of three brides whose weddings had been arranged between one o'clock and three o'clock. As is often the case, the first bride was late. It appeared that in this case she'd opted for a vintage car to convey her to the church and this particular car was so vintage that it had broken down in the middle of the high street, leaving the bride to transfer to a passing mini-cab whose driver had taken her to the wrong church.

Presently the vicar whispered to the choir that he had it on good authority that she was now definitely on her way. Our senior bass, who had ensconced himself at the end of a back pew and was chewing a thick, oozing sandwich with great relish, remarked cheerfully that if she didn't hurry up the lot for the second wedding would be arriving. They'd have to wait, and in turn they'd get mixed up with the third lot. He smiled happily. 'We've seen it all before – absolute chaos. Livens things up no end.'

There was a sudden commotion outside the west door, a flurry of people with cameras, camcorders and complaining children in pushchairs, and the bride arrived supporting a red-faced bewildered looking father and determinedly holding a film-star smile and aiming it in all directions.

The senior bass sandwich-chewer rose quickly, neatly brushing crumbs and bits of corned beef all over the visitors' book on the bookstand, and with a growl or two marshalled the choir into a dignified procession to lead the bride up the aisle to where the vicar stood beaming and eager to get things moving and deliver his favourite number 3 stock wedding homily. (Since the parish church has been chosen for so many more wedding services these days the vicar rotated three stock wedding homilies. He reckoned that it made the whole proceeding far more interesting for him than when he had only one stock wedding homily.)

As soon as we reached 'Praise, my soul, the King of heaven' it was very clear that the bride and groom and most of the congregation were used to our kind of singing and, in fact, were better at it than we were. They just about drowned the choir by the second verse – and until then I'd never come across any other choir that even approached us for sheer uninhibited volume.

During the vicar's number 3 wedding homily the senior bass, noting perhaps that I was looking somewhat shattered, nodded in the direction of the bridal couple. '*They* were both in the other choir,' he explained. 'He left because their vicar stopped them wearing cassocks and surplices and *she* left because she couldn't take her Great Dane into the churchyard anymore.' He scanned the crowded pews. 'Most of their choir are in the congregation,' he confirmed.

'It sounds like it,' I agreed.

'Ah!' he growled. 'It's very quiet at their church now. The congregation won't stand *that* for much longer. They're not used to *that* kind of thing.'

'Do you think that their vicar will change his mind about things, then?' I asked. 'Obviously, he's a New Age vicar. He knows where everybody in the church has been going wrong about everything all these years and he knows exactly how they must put things right.'

'Their choir won't care what age he is as long as he leaves *them* alone,' nodded the bass. 'But in the end their vicar's got to be popular. It's no good being New Age if nobody takes any notice of you

– and you don't get to be popular by taking away people's cassocks and surplices and ripping out windows that people don't want ripped out.'

At this point our vicar finished number 3 stock homily, and slipped in a quick thought that the happy day would be made very much happier for the church cleaner if everyone would wait till they were *outside* the church and not hurl their confetti all over the pews and floor. Then we all finished up with a thunderous rendering of 'Jerusalem' and the congregation smartly shuffled into position to hurl their confetti all over the pews and floor.

And the bass has proved to be correct. The new vicar at the church of the disintegrating choir has recently, reluctantly, recognized his unsuccessful tactics and very sadly compromised. So, for the moment, the choir have stopped disintegrating and carry on as usual, the Victorian windows remain firmly fixed in their multi-coloured splendour, the notice board is innocent of red neon and no one stops the choir dogs and their pals meeting in the churchyard. The removal of the ancient font and the appearance of the new bright chummy refreshment bar is, however, now a reality. The trouble at present is that members of the congregation inveigled into using it after Sunday morning service

still tend to treat the area with their usual reverence and everyone tiptoes about and speaks in whispered, and the lady in charge, being slightly hard of hearing anyway, often has great difficulty in discovering whether a customer wants tea or coffee or is just complaining about the sermon.

5

The Choir Goes West

I was standing behind a piece of scenery, frantically trying to learn two lines written on a tattered envelope which I had carried about for six months. The occasion was a village choir's annual winter show, somewhere in Suffolk. Being well known as a guest member of the choir whenever I visited a relative in that area, I had been invited to take a small part in the show. So there I stood.

On stage, a group of choristers dressed as cowboys sat round an electric light bulb covered with red paper, which was supposed to resemble a fire, but succeeded in looking like a bulb covered with red paper. The cowboys were all shuddering and clutching weighty blankets about themselves as one announced, 'How cold it is on the prairie tonight!'

The acting was quite good, but was somewhat spoilt because a particularly warm night and a particularly well-stoked boiler, allied to no ventilation whatsoever, had turned the village hall into an oven.

One cowboy, perspiration trickling freely down his face, now stood up and suggested that they should all sing to keep warm. This was greeted by much applause and was also my cue to enter. I was the only alto they had, so they were obliged to get me on the stage somehow.

I (who felt ridiculous in a check shirt and ten-gallon hat) strode from behind the scenery and announced urgently, 'There's a rider a-comin' up the trail, he's a-comin mighty fast!' This was followed by the sound of two halves of a coconut being clapped slowly together in a manner suggestive of a very old and tired horse just about staggering to a halt. The newcomer was our principal bass, in the guise of the sheriff, and the singing group was now complete and raring to go.

I can't remember the details of the plot or even why we were all sitting about on the prairie round the electric bulb, but I think we were supposed to be carving an empire out of the wilderness. Characters in Westerns are always carving empires out of the wilderness, and this is usually done by rustling cattle, holding up a stagecoach, or discreetly blasting half a mountainside on someone's head at Dead Man's Gulch. However, as this was supposed to be a musical Western we remained peacefully singing cowboy songs until the interval. The audience really entered into the spirit of the thing, and I was interested to note that they seemed to know the ballads far better than the hymns on Sunday. At any rate, they didn't gape in shocked amazement when anyone sang above a whisper.

During the interval, after the stampede for free tea and biscuits had subsided, the vicar said he was delighted to see so many parishioners enjoying themselves, and hoped that they'd think the choir's efforts were worth a large donation in the plate at the close of the show. As they all knew, the money was to go towards the producing of a new boiler for the hall.

One churchwarden, who by now was almost collapsing with the heat, was heard to suggest that what the hall needed was a refrigerator, but he was always complaining about something and nobody took any notice.

An impossibly ancient lady sitting in the front row then violently demanded of the vicar when they were going to get some action into the play. In the Westerns they had on the telly, she said, people got shot and strung up all over the place. They didn't keep lazing about on the floor.

The vicar started to calm her down in the highly

successful manner in which he dealt with church council members who wanted to get something done. 'Patience, patience,' he crooned, putting his hand on her shoulder. 'All in good time, I am sure.'

Luckily for him the curtain rose at that moment and saved him from a rather nasty situation. The ancient lady was not a member of the church council, and had no intention of being soothed. But she couldn't complain about lack of action in the second half of our epic.

We were now all in the Red Dog Saloon, where a bad man from Arizona way was trying to terrorize the bartender into giving him free whisky. He waved two plastic guns, and spoke with a strong homely Suffolk accent, immediately recognizable as belonging to the choirman who was always a beat behind in the hymns and a tone flat in the psalms.

None of the dozen other customers in the saloon dared to come to the aid of the bartender because the bad man was completely dressed in black, and in the West this is always a sign of real meanness, and no mercy whatsoever. Whether it be a fine upstanding cowboy, or his poor old widowed mother, a badman shoots on the slightest provocation, or on no provocation at all.

The ancient lady in the front row knew all about

this extraordinary type and started to urge the bad man to get on with the killing, but at that vital moment, when it looked as though the bartender would be lucky if he only lost a bottle of his best whisky, the swing doors opened and in fell the hero. He shouldn't have *fallen* in, of course, but he was the choir's tenor soloist, who always performed with closed eyes, and had not therefore noticed a choirboy who was crouching behind the doors, holding them up.

From this point the tables were turned, and things went disastrously for the bad man. Every time he snarled at the hero, that gentleman struck an attitude and started to sing. This so upset the bad man that he could only deflate against the bar and gulp down more free whisky. Certainly the tenor sang convincingly. It was a pity that he was so short and plump, because heroes in Westerns are, of course, always ten feet tall and mighty lean. However, with the aid of confidence and high-heeled boots he managed quite well.

But it was the action that wrung the cheers from the audience. The songs slowed things up. A choir-man remarked afterwards that he'd noted the expressions on the faces of the audience while the hero was singing. They were similar to that worn

by the vicar during the performance of a rather long anthem when he was bursting to get on with the sermon and aim a broadside at some troublesome members of the congregation.

The vicar was like that. He kept everyone up to scratch. As I left the hall that night he was standing at the exit, holding the collection plate a few inches under the nose of a very prominent parishioner. She was an enormously wealthy widow who admitted proudly that since her children's church days she had never failed to put her 'Sunday sixpence' in the bag.

'A very good show, don't you think?' the vicar was saying. 'A *very* good show.' And he pushed the plate closer and fixed her with his beady eye.

6

Take a Pew

'She told me to meet her at the church *sharp* at nine o'clock,' announced Hacksaw. 'She's insisted that it shall be *sharp* at nine o'clock because she's such a busy person, having so many important engagements, and cannot tolerate hanging about waiting for lackadaisical people who can't tell the time.'

On a fine, bright Saturday morning in late spring Hacksaw and I were walking to the village church where he was to meet and receive instructions from a comparative newcomer to the parish, a mother of a bride-to-be who had obviously taken full and firm charge of all arrangements for her daughter's forthcoming wedding service at the church.

I've written previously about my old friend and former woodwork master, Hacksaw. He has been organist and choirmaster at his church forever, leading a choir of whom most (there are some young ones) have been around just as long. All are highly respected and indulged by the vicar, the church council and the whole congregation and are constantly being called upon to sing on all kinds of occasions apart from the regular Sunday services, but especially at the unusually high proportion of wedding services the village church seems to attract. Even the vicar's warden, a dedicated musician of delicate susceptibilities who shudders whenever he even thinks about the choir, freely admits that when you are faced with a village full of people whose main occupation seems to be the arranging of weddings and yours is the only church for miles around that possesses anything that can remotely be referred to as a choir, it pays to hang on tightly to whatever you've got, no matter how much flattery it takes.

We arrived at the church with time to spare but the lady was already there parading back and forth before the porch. I made myself scarce and Hacksaw beamed his oft-practised most welcoming smile and bounded to meet her. She beamed in turn, a large, gushingly friendly lady in a flowing, flowery dress of many hues who was keen to 'look the church over' as a setting for the big wedding. She and her family had never attended the church services or indeed set foot inside the church at all but she declared that it was the *prettiest* church ever and absolutely *made* the village with the historic Fox and Grapes tavern next door to the churchyard and her lovely new Tudor-style house with the *glorious* garden which she had created, just across the path from where she had the most romantic view of the church from her lounge window . . .

She sighed happily as she viewed the sturdy age-battered oak pews for the first time. 'I've seen some like these at antique fairs,' she enthused. 'I keep on telling myself they're *just* the thing I need for garden benches, but they are a good idea for churches too. For the wedding we shall be able to decorate the ends with floral sprays. You can't do that with chairs or tip-up seats.'

She moved up the centre aisle and stopped at the chancel steps peering up at the choirstalls. 'What are these for?' she asked. 'I suppose they're for the high-ups.'

'Yes, members of the choir,' agreed Hacksaw solemnly.

'Ah, yes, we shall want a lot of those to help with the singing.' The lady became businesslike and from a capacious scarlet leather bag fished out a shell-pink writing pad and miniature pencil with a golden tassel. 'Now, the bit where the bride comes in – you know, after the photographers have got their pictures of her arriving at the church in her white Rolls . . .'

'The procession up the aisle,' clarified Hack-saw.

'That's right,' agreed the lady. 'This friend of my daughter got married last year and had the trumpet thing played on the organ. My daughter wants that trumpet thing too.'

'Right,' acquiesced Hacksaw, 'the trumpet thing it shall be.'

And from then on Hacksaw took over. For untold years (everything in Hacksaw's choir has been done for untold years) the choir has had a small rigidly fixed programme of wedding music which they use at all weddings no matter what the wedding participants think they require. Veteran arranger, superb fixer, Hacksaw has a magical, quite devious gift for persuading his clients that they have chosen all their favourite music and that he has enthusiastically agreed with this choice. The lady seemed most pleased and satisfied that she had all her musical instructions agreed to in under twenty minutes and turned briskly to take her leave. In the doorway she turned again. 'Oh, and she wants "Oh, for the wings of a dove" as well,' she announced firmly, and in a billow of colour and exotic perfume she was gone.

I was staying with Hacksaw for a few days and as is our custom at such times I joined him in the choir on Sunday for choral matins. A few minutes before the service was due to start, as the hubbub in the choir vestry rose to its accustomed riotous volume, Hacksaw stood up below a framed notice on the wall which counselled in Gothic letters of gold 'Compose yourselves for worship' and shouted, 'Shut up, you lot! Now just watch it in the anthem, and basses, *do* try to be a bit more friendly with each other and come in together, not one behind the other ... and by all means all of you sing "Stand up, stand up for Jesus" as if you're enjoying it but don't go berserk and try to drown the vicar. You know you can't do it once he gets going and he can't *help* being tone-deaf, so don't try to drown him, however much he deserves it.'

And, as usual, on he went with his good advice of which, as usual, no one appeared to take the slightest notice. Finally he butted into an intriguing discussion between three choirgirls about the merits and demerits of someone's latest hairdo and advised one of them, 'Gloria, don't arrange anything for the last Saturday in June. We've got another "Wings of a dove" wedding.'

Gloria, who always sang the solo at weddings (it was on Hacksaw's 'optional extras' list) and had a most attractive voice and, in the eyes of the young male members of the choir, was altogether most attractive, tossed back her silver blonde mane. 'Who is it this time?' she asked. 'Last time it was that girl from the post office who kept on crying all the time I was singing.'

Hacksaw regarded his charming soprano with pride. 'She said afterwards that your singing brought tears to her eyes,' he said. 'That was a great compliment. Not everyone can make a girl so happy that she cries at her own wedding. Anyway, this next bride won't cry when you sing. Her mother won't let her. She's Mrs Whatsername's girl. Her at the Tudor house across the road.'

Gloria was studying herself in the vestry mirror. 'Nice girl,' she said. 'I was at school with her in our last term. I never thought she'd get married, though. She would keep taking her boyfriends home to see her mother and no one stayed after that.'

'Are we ready, choir?' came the vicar's anxious voice and we all formed up and shuffled into church.

I was not in the village again till some weeks after the big wedding had come and gone but on a fine, misty, warm late summer Sunday morning I was again making my way through the churchyard to join Hacksaw's choir for choral matins. Near the vestry door I came upon the 'Wings of a dove' soprano perched elegantly among the angels and cherubs on the flamboyant Manor House tomb, talking to Cranmer, the vicar's cat, a splendid, hefty black and white moggy of commanding presence who sat under the pulpit during the services but disapproved of long sermons, always walking out, tail erect, right down the middle aisle if the vicar went on beyond ten minutes.

'You look *most* decorative!' I greeted her enthusiastically, and Cranmer swished his tail in agreement.

'If Hacksaw spies me he'll say I'm making the churchyard look untidy and start going on about the younger generation,' she sparkled.

'He's got no soul,' I said. 'But tell me, how did the big wedding go?'

'Oh, it was quiet,' she said, 'very quiet.'

'Very *quiet*?' I queried incredulously. 'Quiet?' Cranmer opened wide his brilliant green eyes and looked expectantly from one to the other of us.

This looked as though it might be interesting. He sat up alertly and purred.

'Well, you know how it is,' Gloria went on, 'nowadays people who are regular churchgoers generally barge into church before the service and start tramping all over the place chattering and shaking hands and hugging each other as if they've not seen each other for ages, and making the whole place look like a mainline railway station at the height of the rush hour.'

'So . . . ?' I began.

'But non-churchgoers are different,' she said. 'Non-churchgoers are far more reverent. They drop their voices to a whisper immediately they enter a church and start gliding about on tiptoe and vaguely bowing to anyone in a cassock – and nearly all *that* wedding lot were non-churchgoers. So it was a quiet wedding.'

'But after seeing the organizing lady, I thought . . .' I began.

'And anyway,' she rattled on regardless, 'they were all quite confused with the floral decorations. I imagine they thought they'd strayed into a seriously over-stocked garden centre. The church was so crammed with flowers and tubs of outsized plants that people could hardly get through the doorway.

Then they had quite a job forging their way up the aisle and trying to avoid the thickest of the greenery. Up in the choir we couldn't see the congregation at all because the choir screen had been used to stake up all kinds of monster shrubbery. When I came to do "Oh, for the wings of a dove" I found myself singing to three gorgeous giant sunflowers. They had big round cheerful faces and, do you know, they looked as though they were thoroughly enjoying my efforts. It was most encouraging.'

Gloria heaved the black and white bulk of Cranmer on to her lap. 'He enjoyed the wedding in a quiet way too,' she said. 'He sat on the edge of the pulpit and kept on knocking lumps of potting compost from an overstuffed hanging basket on to the bride's mother's hat – a thing like a sunshade with ribbons and roses on it.'

Quiet wedding or not, the bride's mother had been ecstatic. Congratulating Hacksaw on all the lovely music, she said she particularly enjoyed listening to it seated in a *pew* instead of on a chair. She'd so loved the pew that she insisted on the vicar selling her one for the garden so he gave her one as a present, a spare one that had been knocking about in the church hall for ages. She was so grateful there were tears in her eyes. 'They can say what they like about registry office weddings,' she declared. 'You can't beat a church wedding!'

7

It's Great!

In a delightful rural parish that I know well, the mere mention of the matins congregation makes the vicar so depressed that he has to shut himself in his study and play soothing Tudor church music, or go for a long lonely walk along the Grand Union Canal.

The matins congregation are quite dreadful. They never were very helpful, but now they've grown absolutely defiant. They refuse to support the vicar's new 'Great Family Service' (anything that the vicar plans is always called 'Great') which takes place at half past nine every Sunday morning, and they *will* keep on coming to matins at eleven o'clock. In vain does the vicar preach to them about the great feeling of unity and community they would enjoy if they came to the Great Family Service. In turn his sermons on the subject have been sorrowful, sarcastic and seething, wheedling, wily and woeful, but it makes no difference: the matins congregation still sit there Sunday after Sunday in the same pews where they've sat for years. And they just look through him and take no notice at all.

Luckily for the vicar they are not interested in being on the church council. They never appear near the church on weekdays, and only read the church magazine in church on Sundays while they are waiting for matins to begin.

The only exception is my Uncle Fred. He is a staunch member of the matins congregation, but he also goes to *all* the meetings in the parish, and he is very good at picking holes in everybody else's suggestions and voting against everything. He says it's a free country and we all have a right to speak our minds without fear or favour, and if the vicar thinks he has a monopoly of ideas and is always right he has another thing coming.

Somehow everybody seems to like my Uncle Fred, and they depend on him for many things apart from prolonging church council meetings until the early hours and writing unanswerable letters to the magazine. He is very good at bodging up the church's lethal electrical installation and is, in fact, the only one who has the faintest idea of how to deal with it. He knows, for instance, how to run three electric heaters and the light over the lectern from one small plug, and he is always successful in repairing it when it catches fire. He is in constant demand to attend the organ-blowing motor when the organist, who appears to be deaf, regularly blows the fuse by pulling out all the stops and playing Wagner grand marches for half an hour before each service.

He is also adept at arranging the Great Annual Winter Sale (in the previous vicar's day it was just called the Annual Winter Sale) which is always a great success. For months beforehand Uncle Fred organizes a very efficient collection of old coats, worn-out boots, broken bikes, teapots with no lids and weighty books of Victorian sermons. And on the day of the sale Uncle Fred and the vicar are on the most friendly terms. The vicar gives generous assistance by arranging a Great Opening Ceremony by a Great Favourite of television, films and radio whom no one has ever heard of, and Uncle Fred always greets the Great Favourite with a few well-chosen words that last for about half an hour.

The customers simply fight to get into the church hall. (The sale used to be in the vicarage, but the vicar's wife got a little upset at her brasses continually disappearing off the sideboard and her Great-Uncle Sebastian's mahogany eight-day clock being sold off the mantelpiece by over-enthusiastic members of the Young Wives' Fellowship for fifty pence.) They all carry large canvas bags, and some even suitcases, and these they fill to capacity. Some are so eager to secure the bargains that they quite forget to pay in the general confusion, but Uncle Fred is always on the door with a cheery reminder and his outsized Irish wolfhound.

To increase the cheery communal atmosphere, a churchwarden brings along his home-made radiogram and plays records of happy carefree music, which he has to turn up very loud so that they can be heard above the roar of polite conversation and the refined insults that fill the hall when someone has managed to carry away a genuine battered Victorian brass fender under the very nose of someone else who had reserved it, or when a customer's charming little lad has just experimented with a hastily erected shelf on the provision stall and hurtled three dozen bottles of home-made nettle wine all over the Colonel's old prints and works-of-art stall.

And at the end of the day comes the final, thrilling action. Uncle Fred organizes that too. The idea here seems to be to play on the keeping-up-with-the-Joneses yearning which is so deeply implanted in most humans – at least in most humans who go to my Uncle Fred's sale. If the person next to you has managed to procure a large mass of utterly useless rubbish for next to nothing, then it is up to you to procure at least a similar amount of utterly useless rubbish and, if possible, just that little bit more.

Uncle Fred stands on a table, waving an auctioneer's hammer. For half an hour he doesn't stop talking. Everyone gapes at him, mesmerized. Even the man with the radiogram forgets to put on another record. And when he finally descends from the table into a chaos of home-made sweet wrappings, dropped gloves and bawling mislaid infants, everything in the hall has to be sold.

The matins congregation never come to the Great Annual Winter Sale. They don't want to be happy and carefree and bubbling over with community spirit. They just want to go on sitting in their pews at matins on Sunday and finding out what other futile ruses the vicar has devised to lure them along to the Great Family Service.

But they *do* show an interest in my Uncle Fred – after all, he is one of them – and on the Sunday after the sale quite a number of them can be observed, nodding to him and making genteel remarks such as 'So you had another nice sale then. Good. Good', or 'The results must be *most* gratifying to you. How *good* of you', or 'How on earth you manage even to go *near* that ghastly mob I shall never understand'.

And Uncle Fred beams contentedly.

8

Where Am I?

It was all very well for my daughter to present me with a map as I started out on my recent walking holiday. What I sorely needed was someone to *read* the map. I have never been able to find my way very far at all by maps. And this time I was on my own, somewhere in the West Country. I'd been walking for hours and hours and had seen no one and nothing but the wandering path that I traversed more and more slowly when I realized that I had no idea where I was. With the July midday sun beating down on me in a most threatening way and my small backpack relentlessly turning itself into a ton weight I suddenly slithered into a hidden dry ditch, tumbled over my tired feet and ever so slowly pulled my way up through the midst of a blackberry bush. And there it was – a small stone church with a squat castellated tower that had surely been there for ever, all golden in the sunlight with a huge Shire horse chomping contentedly in the tidy flowery churchyard.

Fatigue forgotten, I made towards the porch hoping the church was open, on the way pausing to have a word with the horse who regarded me for a few moments with a kindly thoughtful expression and gently returned to his grass.

The church *was* open. In the welcome coolness I dropped into a back pew and looked about me. It was an ancient barn wherein a few refinements had transformed it into a house of God. Unique. Wonderful. Presently there came a clattering of footsteps up in the chancel behind the choir screen and a man appeared from the organ. He seemed in no hurry, moving up and down the choirstalls sliding hymnbooks and psalters about and tidying various ragged piles of sheet music. Then he saw me and ambled down the aisle towards me, a middle aged, rotund, jolly looking man wearing a baggy shapeless summer suit and billowing white shirt. 'It's no good telling them,' he said. 'They will *not* put the music away tidy-like – stuff left all over the place after the service and then they wonder why they can't find it the next Sunday. The same with their cassocks and surplices – never put them back on their right pegs and then what a fuss when they've got each other's things on!'

He ruffled his sparse hair. 'I don't know – they've

always been the same. I've been organist here for thirty years and I've never known them to be different. They'll go on being the same for ever, I reckon.'

'The choir?' I hazarded.

'Ah,' he said, 'the choir.'

'I know what you mean,' I said. 'I'm a chorister.'

'Ah!' he said again. 'I thought you were – you *look* like one.' He moved a toppling pile of *Ancient and Modern* hymnals out of the way along a church-warden's pew and we sat and contemplated our lofty surroundings of ancient peace. Presently he produced a tea flask from under the seat. 'I do a bit of tidying up in the churchyard once a week,' he said, 'and run through a few things on the organ – and the tea comes in handy. Here – have a cup. Of course,' he explained pouring some villainously dark, stewed liquid into a plastic cup, 'the choir weren't always down in the front there in the chancel. In the old days they used to be out of the way up in the gallery at the back. We've only been down in the front for about 150 years, but it's getting a sort of a custom now. We've got lots of customs here . . . Well, the business about the choir – it was like this . . .' I sat back, cautiously tackling the tea, and listened . . .

In the early nineteenth century the gallery of the church was the popular, much used exclusive domain of the choir and musicians. No member of the congregation, or even the rector, was encouraged to venture up there and from the body of the church below nobody could see what went on up there. But no matter if the choir didn't wear 'Sunday best', or played dominoes during the sermon, or went outside for a smoke or indulged in any other favourite pastime or simply went to sleep, when it came to 'making a joyful noise unto the Lord' they were superb, unsurpassed and as long as the music of the hymns and psalms rolled from the gallery each Sunday in vigorous full volume to lead the congregation the powers-that-be were quite happy and would doubtless have agreed with the celebrated Victorian actress who is reputed to have declared 'I don't mind what people do as long as they don't do it in the street and frighten the horses.'

But, of course, nothing lasts for ever, and everything changed for the choir when, in the prevailing fashion later in the century, the musicians – a fiddler and a flautist – were replaced by an organ installed down in the chancel, and the choir were brought down from the gallery to be accommodated in choirstalls next to the organ and in full view of the entire congregation.

The choir took up their new position with mixed feelings. Although most members rather fancied the new dark-red cassocks with starched surplices that they were now obliged to wear, they felt hampered and restricted by the realization that they could no longer carry on with their normal practices during the non-singing parts of the service. After all, you could hardly play dominoes during the sermon with the whole front row of the congregation gawping at you, neither could you read the Sunday papers or tramp out to have a smoke. You couldn't really go to sleep during the sermon, at least not until you'd made sure that all the gawpers in the front row of the congregation were already asleep.

But help was at hand. The father of the landlord of the Dog and Duck tavern, which was much patronized by the choir, eventually died aged 102 years and to celebrate his long, adventurous career – mostly wrangling horses, arguing vitriolically on the church council and poaching – his family decided on a monument in the shape of a choir screen, a hefty flamboyant affair of gilded oak that effectually hid the choir once again from the prying eyes of the congregation.

The choir screen has been there for over a century now and is a firmly established favourite with the members of the choir who still carry on as their early Victorian forebears in a manner that has become a revered tradition. Of course, in recent years the screen has evoked the criticism and even downright hostility of one or two forward-thinking vicars who wanted it removed as an iniquitous barrier dividing the united Christian family – apart from being Victorian, a circumstance which always terribly upsets modern forward-thinking vicars. But the congregational part of the united Christian family have always made it abundantly clear that they feel quite united enough without having to look at the choir and their goings on for hours every Sunday. They are all right to listen to, quite good in fact (as long as they don't get out of hand in the more bloodthirsty bits of the psalms), but this is no reason for having to *look* at them ... And so the screen and the choir remain, traditional, unassailable.

To the uninitiated this clinging to tradition in the Church often suggests a dull, moribund state of affairs. How untrue! Beneath the surface of the average parish there is enough intrigue of conflicting aims, revolutionary ideas and downright anarchy to keep the Church vigorously alive and kicking for as long as the 'coffee and chat after the service' tradition flourishes. For instance, there is always someone on the parochial church council who keeps on using such phrases as 'dragging the Church screaming into the twenty-first century' and 'reform or perish', and regularly requests – nay, demands – that the powers-that-be change the hymnbook and sack the organist or rip out all the pews and turn the churchyard into a skateboard park for the kiddies. Recently one such gentleman turned his attention to the re-lighting of the choir-stalls. Originally they had been lighted by candles which, three quarters of a century ago, had been replaced by electric candles. These had generally proved popular with the choir, particularly in recent years with the boys who during the less jolly parts of the vicar's latest, New Age family services, liked to tip the candle-shades in all directions or take them off and replace them upside down so that at the end of the service the chancel always gave the distinct impression that it had been hit by a hurricane or a violent pub brawl.

But these days the choir have lost their electric candles and are now lighted by a series of little spotlights mounted on chrome rods suspended over the stalls and well out of reach of even he most athletic choirboys. Nevertheless, the chrome rods don't do much to enhance the ancient beauty of their surroundings and the lights themselves are as superfluous as were the electric candles because, as the organist explained, the choir never find it necessary to consult their music. They know by heart all the hymns and psalms that are used and the 'pot boiler' anthems which they alternate throughout the year. The practice of holding their music up before them while singing is really the organist's idea. He says it gives the choir something to do with their hands and it looks uniform and sort of professional.

'And that,' said the organist, 'brings me almost up to date with the story of our choir . . . almost.'

'I'm in no hurry if you're not,' I assured him.

He nudged the threatening pile of *Ancient and Moderns* a little further along the pew and settled back comfortably again. 'Well,' he continued, 'we've got a newcomer in the congregation – they crop up now and again, you know, and they've generally got a sort of mission, a burning desire to get into the life of the local church and invigorate and trans-form it by altering everything they can lay their

hands on. This lady could be any age, I suppose –
she reminds me of a cheeky sparrow – and she
keeps on shouting about all over the place and
making "vital statements" and writing to the parish
magazine and waylaying the vicar with urgent
appeals against everything from the vestry drainage
system to the vicar's dilapidated outdoor attire.
And above all she says the choir's chrome lights
must go. She says they are the final vandalization
of a noble building. She adds that the choir screen
and the choir themselves are, of course, other van-
dalizations but the lights are the last straw. Lately
she's consolidated her plans that deem it essential
that the lights and the screen and the choir are
removed and she has generously volunteered to
organize a team of parishioners to clean up the
gallery and make the floor safe, so that the choir
can be put back well out of sight where they came
from.'

'Whatever will happen?' I asked aghast.

'Oh, we're not worried in the choir,' he said
easily. 'Our present vicar is a very astute man and
very experienced. The whisper is that he's about to
invite the lady to join the parochial church council.
At their meetings they talk for hours and hours and
she will be able to let off steam for as long as she

wants. I've known them to talk till after midnight. They really enjoy themselves in a nice relaxed atmosphere in the vicar's study.'

'Do they act promptly on their deliberations?' I asked.

'Deliberations?' he repeated puzzled. 'Oh, they don't have many of those. Oh, no. Very cautious are the parochial church council, very civilized. They seldom rock the boat.'

'Ah,' I nodded.

'And that *does* bring us up to date,' beamed the organist, reaching under the pew for some more villainous tea. We moved out into the churchyard. 'Now when you're this way again,' he invited, 'you must come and sing in the choir. Just turn up in the vestry and we'll fit you up with a cassock and surplice.' He realized that he was still holding his plastic cup of black tea. He regarded it with surprise and some doubt and neatly tipped it into some bushes. We shook hands and he disentangled a somewhat rusty bike from the bushes and peddled away up a winding lane.

'Oh, I say,' I called after him urgently. 'Do you mind telling me where . . .' – but he'd rounded a bend and was gone.

The Shire horse continued to chomp happily.

Yes, I certainly *would* return and sing in the choir – wherever they might be in the church. If only I knew where I was . . .

9

The Organization

The friend with whom I was staying had told me that the village church was very much alive. 'We don't have a lot of separate organizations,' he had explained. 'We have a pool of labour and the vicar organizes us into doing everything from stoking the boiler to singing in the choir. Of course, most of us can't stoke or sing, but that doesn't matter. We're organized.'

As I approached the church, a young man with a very intelligent expression behind a red beard and horn-rimmed glasses was studiously hacking away at the graveyard hedge with a vicious-looking bill-hook. Every time he struck the hedge it sprang back at him and, apart from shedding a few leaves, remained exactly as it was. Just inside the gate another man was up a tree. He balanced on top of a ladder that was firmly wedged against a dead branch which he appeared to be sawing off. On a stretch of grass between some tombstones a boy wearing an indescribably filthy choir ruffle was galloping about at a frightening pace with a lawnmower. Presently it skidded to a halt so suddenly that it threw him headlong over the handlebars. He didn't seem to mind in the slightest, but was merely puzzled by the fact that the machine would no longer turn after being driven over half a brick.

Inside the church the same enthusiasm met me. On a sagging plank suspended between high trestles, two large gentlemen in shirt sleeves and immaculate pin-striped trousers were sloshing generous quantities of whitewash around – and across – the clerestory windows. Below them a very business-like lady was violently polishing a most superior-looking lectern eagle with what appeared to be a red-and-white football jersey full of holes. Three very small birdlike ladies were fluttering all over the place doing things with jam-jars and bunches of languishing golden rod; standing on tiptoe on an umbrella-stand, a youth sporting outsized rubber boots was busy replacing light bulbs and leaving some fine and rather decorative sets of fingerprints in the dust on the tasteful dinner-plate type shades. And in the back pew, proudly watching the joyous activity, reclined the vicar. The vicar was a very good organizer.

I don't think I could have been looking active enough because as soon as he spotted me he directed me to report to the vestry where a certain Mr Brown would fix me up with a job. I explained gently that I was a visitor and didn't particularly want Mr Brown to fix me up with job just then, whereupon the vicar took a second look at me, obviously decided that I was not the kind of material from which successful pools of labour are made, and immediately lost interest. However, he kindly suggested that if I didn't object to a bit of dirt and a little exertion, I might like to climb to the top of the church tower. The tower was open to the public each evening during the summer and was in charge of the oldest member of the congregation, dear old Egbert. 'No matter what their age, everyone *does* something in this parish,' he said.

As I peeped into the dark doorway of the tower a gentleman who looked uncannily like a cross and ancient eagle pounced from under the stairs and grated, 'pound admittance'. Dear old Egbert was certainly keen on his job. He dropped my coin into a large tin with a slit in the lid, and said he couldn't understand why anyone wanted to go up the filthy tower unless they *had* to. Now, take him, for instance. He *had* to. It was his job to look after the bells and clear out the dead pigeons and wind the clock. (Very tricky the clock was, and wouldn't work for just anybody.) He was, in fact, the steeple-keeper. Of course, there wasn't any steeple these days, only the tower, but the title had been handled down from the days when there had been one. On a stormy night in 1890 it had fallen through the chancel roof and completely demolished the organ on which, rumour had it, Handel had once tried to play.

Dear old Egbert prodded me before him up the narrow, winding, pitch-dark stairway. He apologized for not having a torch and gave an explanation. I think it was something about having lost it the previous night when he was looking for his cat in the blackcurrant bushes. I only fell over three times and he said I was pretty good for a stranger.

As I negotiated the tiny exit to the roof of the tower, I just failed to duck low enough to avoid cracking my head on an unsuspected beam. A burst of spontaneous good-hearted laughter rocked dear old Egbert. He said it was always interesting to see just how hard people would bump themselves up there. Most of them were in such a hurry to get aloft that they nearly knocked themselves out. I'd been lucky taking it more steadily. Still, he couldn't help laughing. He became even more charming when we stood on top of the tower. He invited me to look down over the parapet at a spot where, in my ignorance, I thought I could see a great mass of rubble and defiant-looking weeds. He said it was one of the finest rock gardens in the county and he'd done it all himself. Only after I'd been hanging over the parapet in speechless bewilderment for some minutes did he casually mention that if he were me he wouldn't *lean* so much because the parapet was quiet unsafe. In fact, he didn't know how it stood there at all. The vicar was organizing something soon.

When I had sufficiently recovered, I thanked him for his kindness and made to depart. But the tour wasn't over. Apparently it included some thumbnail sketches of the local celebrities who could be spotted from our vantage point. For example, there went the chairman of the church council. Not a good type at all. Had been the ringleader in stopping a gentleman who wanted to bring progress to the village by building a nice big concrete petrol station in front of the church. And could I see the curate? Didn't earn his money, he didn't. Only gave ten-minute sermons and even had to *read* those. As for the crowd of characters rolling out of the Fox and

Ferret, they were the bellringers and they ought to be locked up. Made such a row on Sunday mornings that you had to be stone deaf to sleep after half-past ten.

Suddenly dear old Egbert grabbed my arm and pointed excitedly to a figure striding up the church path. 'And he's the worst of the lot!' he whispered with a certain awesome reverence. 'He won't do what the vicar tells him! Does what he likes!'

'He's not even in the pool of labour?' I queried.

'No!'

'Then he *must* be the organist,' I said.

Dear old Egbert regarded me with a new interest.

'How did you know?' he asked.

10

Just Call Me Butch

As usual after Sunday matins in Doc Brown's incredibly ancient village church, the adult members of the choir had drifted into Doc Brown's incredibly ancient village pub. It is the custom to call both establishments Doc Brown's because he is both the longstanding organist of the church and the longstanding landlord of the pub and manages both very well. It is known that he is not a doctor of medicine and I don't think he can be a doctor of music, but nobody ever calls him anything but Doc Brown.

On this fine July Sunday morning I'd joined the members in the tavern as I'd come from the station for a few days' break in the village, which would include lending a hand in the choir at evensong with what the Doc called a hoot or two in the alto line.

'Now when I was a choirboy . . .' he commenced, moving behind the bar.

'Here we go again,' announced our soprano soloist, a teenage choirgirl of much charm and cheek and flamboyant attire, who was dragging the pub's huge tabby cat on to her lap. 'We know the whole story. When you were a choirboy you had no silly women in the choir mucking up everything. You just had men and horrible little boys mucking up everything.'

'Hold your tongue, hussy,' ordered the Doc. 'Listen and learn. When I was a choirboy parishioners always called the vicar "Vicar" or "Mr So-and So", and across the way at the high church they called him "Father So-and-So".'

'Nice and formal,' put in the larger of our two large basses, accepting a foaming tankard from Doc Brown. 'People were formal. Showed respect.'

'But nowadays, what do we get?' went on the Doc.

'No respect,' boomed the larger bass.

'Exactly! Exactly!' pursued the Doc. 'Nowadays everything has to be informal.'

'Friendly,' put in the choirgirl.

'Shut up, you,' said the Doc. 'Showing any respect for a vicar's – er –'

'Vocation,' supplied the larger bass.

'Yes, that,' agreed the Doc. 'That's all old hat

76

these days. You're supposed to be all chummy and call him just by his Christian name – and not even that now. To be *really* in the swim it has to be his *shortened* Christian name – or his nickname.'

'Ever so friendly, that is,' said the choirgirl. 'I always call people by their nicknames and they call me . . .'

'Can't you go off somewhere and practise your solo for evensong, or help your Mum with the washing-up?' suggested the Doc.

'I know my solo, and Mum's *done* the washing-up,' argued the choirgirl. 'My Mum *always* does the washing-up.'

'So nowadays,' continued the Doc heavily, 'we have Father Chris, Father Steve and Father Ben – or just Chris, Steve and Ben – and whereas us choirboys used to call the vicar "Sir", we now have hooligans like our lot here bawling across the vestry things like "'Ere, Ben, someone's pinched my cassock!"'

'Someone's always having a cassock pinched,' confirmed the choirgirl. 'I've sewn my name in mine.'

'Man of the cloth,' recited a tall, aesthetic-looking young man, the choir's solo alto, as he draped himself along the back of the ancient settle where the body of the choir members had gathered. 'A lovely sounding phrase, I always think, but we don't hear it so much these days. But I suppose that's understandable, really, as Fathers Chris, Steve and Ben seem to shun clerical garb in favour of sportswear, jeans and T-shirts except when they're actually conducting a service. And the priestly dog collar has shrunk to a small strip of white plastic which is shoved into the shirt collar and removed as soon as the service is over.'

'It's happening all over, of course. You've got to admit it,' said the larger bass. 'This fashion for informality is spreading and flourishing, not only in the church but absolutely everywhere.'

'That's right,' agreed the choirgirl, stroking the purring bulk of the tabby. 'Alfie here is down as Alfred on his record card at the vet's, but no one ever calls him anything but Alfie – and *he* doesn't like wearing a collar either.'

'I don't know why I put up with you,' confessed the Doc.

'Because I can sing,' countered the choirgirl. 'And you like me, really. Anyway, I'm hungry and lunch isn't for ages. Why don't you buy me a pie?'

'If I buy you a pie, will you go away until evensong?' pleaded the Doc.

'No,' said the choirgirl.

The Doc passed her a pie.

In the vestry, where later that day the choir were gathering for evensong, a fledgling bachelor curate, an enthusiastic disciple of the informal school, was beaming at the choirgirl and addressing her as 'Gorgeous', and she was responding by calling him 'Tubby' – which he was, being a happy, contented young man who existed on enormous quantities of cream cakes and chips with everything else, and whose only exercise appeared to be the occasional walk to the other end of the village to visit the local octogenarian when he couldn't get a lift there or the octogenarian decided not to meet him halfway to the Red Lion.

Suddenly espying me, the young man excused himself from Gorgeous and bounced across with outstretched hands. 'Ah, it's the Doc's friend from Surrey – Reg, yes, Reg – or Reggie, perhaps?' He confessed that he was called Tubby and was a 'new boy' around the place and that Barry (the vicar) who was preaching at a neighbouring church had told him I'd be popping in for evensong. He waved his hands expansively over the assembled company as if taking in at least the rest of the world – Sid and Ida, Bill, Butch, Thumper, Edie, Gorgeous –

well, of course, I knew them all, yes. Anyway, we'd better get going with the service now seeing it had gone half past six. And with a final all-embracing grin over the choir and a moment's pause for the vestry prayer, which was always recited at such speed that no one ever knew what it was about, we all processed into the chancel.

It seemed to me that the congregation was larger than I remembered from previous visits, and almost immediately I had my view confirmed by our second largest bass, who nodded down at the well-filled pews and informed me 'First Sunday the new bloke's been on his own here. *They've* all turned up to see that he doesn't start mucking about with the service and twisting things back to front, like these new men generally try to. You have to be on the watch all the time. No sooner have you broken in a new vicar than you've got to start all over again with a new curate.'

However, the young man in question so far seemed to be giving no cause for complaint and joined in heartily with our favourite hymns, which were always chosen by the Doc for their good rousing tunes, irrespective of the sense or nonsense of the words. Then, in the pulpit, the new curate looked really happy and at home. He said he was looking forward with great pleasure to the time when he had visited the whole congregation and had really got to know everyone. He'd already met Ginger (the verger), who had taken him around the church and shown him where everything was, or was supposed to be, and he'd had interesting chats with Bert and Sid, Bill and Thumper, and most other members of the choir in the Bird in Hand and the Red Lion. And Madge and Pearl had put him right about the Women's Fellowship and, of course, little Rosemary and Claude and Francine, the leading lights in the Sunday School, although they hadn't said much to him, were obviously tickled pink to welcome him to their play last night about Daniel in the lions' den. He had also met Clanger, the captain of the bellringers, who had found out from Pam and Fran (the coffee ladies) that it was his birthday next Sunday and had suggested a three-hour celebration peal after lunch ... people had been most kind.

The second largest bass growled at me again. 'It's all very well, all this Christian name and nickname business, but what about Christmas?'

'Christmas?' I repeated.

'Yes, how about addressing Christmas cards? He doesn't seem to know anyone's surname. Hardly the thing to receive an envelope with just Madge or Butch on it, is it?'

Back in Doc Brown's incredibly ancient pub after evensong, the choir members had been ensconced in their usual places on and around the ancient settle for the best part of an hour and the topic was still that of the ever-encroaching tide of informality in the church, as represented locally by the new curate. So engrossed were they that they didn't notice the arrival of the subject of their discussion until he spoke. 'Thought it was time I introduced *him* to you all,' the new curate announced, indicating a cheerful-looking brown and white hound of uncertain pedigree, with huge paws and thrashing tail, who skirmished at the end of a thick short lead. 'He arrived yesterday – a present from my sister who's worried that I'm not getting enough exercise. I reckon he's already walked me a hundred miles. I'm just about ready to drop.'

He really didn't look as though he was in danger of dropping, and with one accord we gathered admiringly around his splendid beast, who was frantically making friends with us all with tongue and paw.

'Now that's a *real* dog,' averred the larger bass. 'What's his name? Patch?'

The young man looked almost affronted. 'Patch? He was born on Trafalgar Day,' he said. 'His name is Lord Nelson.'

11

In Passing

I moved noiselessly along a soft earth path towards the cosy, slumbering village church which I'd suddenly come upon during a walking holiday in Oxfordshire. It was early afternoon on a warm, quiet August day. In the stillness the tiny sounds of insects in the tall, dry churchyard grass enhanced a deep, remote peace. I peeped into the cool dimness of the church. Silence. I stepped inside and closed the huge door soundlessly and found myself tiptoeing up the aisle. If I'd had a companion with me, I'd have been whispering 'Isn't this delightful?' At that moment of ancient calm I was certainly not expecting the Grand March from *Aida*, but that was what it was. It burst forth from the organ with all the power of its pomp and splendour and continued flamboyantly to its climax. Its final chords rolled regally round the church and dissolved into an utter silence, as if they had never been.

Moments later a shuffling came from the organ

and the sound of a jaunty male voice singing 'Woman is fickle'. The singer – an elderly, rotund, cheerful-faced man – materialized in the choirstalls and immediately spotted me.

'I enjoyed the voluntary,' I enthused.

'For a wedding at four o'clock,' beamed the organist. 'Very nice for getting out of the church with after the ceremony. You need something a bit longer than the old Mendelssohn wedding march these days. The couple can't just walk out straight down the aisle like they used to. Nowadays people jump out of them from pews and from behind pillars and from under the font with cameras and loads of video equipment and until the happy pair have grinned and giggled to everyone's satisfaction they can't get out of church. I've often had to play the Grand March twice before we've finally got rid of them and sometimes even then I've had to slip in "Moonlight and roses".'

Observing my interest in the organ, the organist warmed to the subject and invited me to look at the console. It was obvious that the instrument was well looked after and that the oak case was very fine indeed. 'It's called the Stopper Organ,' he explained. 'It was given late last century by a man who made a lot of money making stoppers for beer bottles. There's a memorial plaque to him behind the radiator in the vestry.'

Sitting in the choirstalls we enjoyed a most interesting half-hour chat about organists and choirs and their traditional difficulties with the contrariness of backward-looking old vicars and forward-looking young ones, until the organist suddenly noticed the time and hastily rose. 'The wedding!' he reminded himself. 'People will be poking around in here soon. I'm sorry to rush away . . .' A sudden thought struck him. 'I wonder . . .' he speculated. 'You're a choir man, you say. I don't suppose you'd help us out by coming in the choir for this wedding? We're going to be awfully short. We're right in the middle of the holiday season and a lot of our choir people are away. What do you say?'

I said I'd be absolutely delighted to help out. 'There's nothing I'd like better,' I assured him. 'By the way, I'm an alto.'

'Never mind,' he encouraged. 'Most of the stuff we're doing will be in unison.'

He took me into the vestry, which was a curtained-off space behind the organ filled with what looked like the unsuccessful remains of half-a-dozen jumble sales packed into half-a-dozen large cardboard boxes. They overflowed with old cardigans, odd shoes, coat hangers and a variety of battered kettles and saucepans. The organist said there'd just be time to make us a cup of tea, and from under a historic sink full of flower vases and milk bottles he dislodged a kettle, infinitely more battered than the jumble sale leftovers, which he filled from a huge dripping brass tap and placed on a gas ring on what I imagined was the vicar's desk. From a row of mugs ranged along the top of the vestry piano – a forbidding black monster with elephantine legs – he selected two as big as jam jars, which were both presents from somewhere or other, and in no time at all we were sitting on a large dusty table (there being no discernible chairs in the place) enjoying what was to me at least a very welcome cup of tea.

We were soon disturbed. Choir members now started arriving and rummaging behind us on the table among what I thought was just another pile of jumble sale leavings. This pile, however, proved to be the choir's robes and it was quite fascinating to see how quickly each member disentangled his or her robes and deftly donned them. A total of half-a-dozen singers eventually turned up – four men and two ladies. After the organist had introduced me to them as a kind of wandering minstrel and had fitted me out in a voluminous candle-grease-encrusted cassock and a choirboy's surplice, we were ready for the wedding.

Although the time was four o'clock there seemed to be no sense of urgency. In the manner of brides this one had not yet arrived, and in any case the vicar, who was doubtless very used to the ways of brides, hadn't arrived either. He was a keen gardener, the organist explained, and his practice was to continue what he was doing in his garden until he spotted the bride arriving, and then quickly to enter the vestry, don his surplice – he gardened in his cassock – comb his hair and be ready, all smiles and fertilizer fumes, well before the photographers had finished with the bride at the front of the church.

Everything went well on that fine summer afternoon. The choir met the bride at the door and led her up the aisle to the strains of a marvellous piece of music which the organist made to sound like that from a steam roundabout organ. It was composed by a Frenchman late last century and reflected, I thought, the composer's admiration for Offenbach's can-can.

The first hymn was that puzzling wedding favourite, Blake's 'Jerusalem'. Most people I've spoken to on the subject are rather hazy as to what Blake was getting at and have no idea at all how the hymn especially applies to a wedding anyway, but it seems to have been drummed into schoolchildren for years and years so that in later life, if they are not churchgoers, it's the first thing that enters their heads when the word 'hymn' is mentioned. Certainly the large congregation sang the words lustily, including the mothers of the bride and groom, although in their case maybe concentration on singing was more than a little distracted by the fact that they had obviously realized that they were wearing identical hats.

As the service progressed a very friendly choirman next to me kept offering me throat-sweets and a continuous series of thumbnail sketches of the wedding party personalities in the congregation. Between the first hymn and the making of the vows I learned, among many other things, that the bride's father was in a shocking mood because he had been overruled and the reception was to be held in the village hall instead of the bar of the Red Lion as he had proposed, and that the bridegroom was so embarrassed and humiliated at the thought of appearing in public in a suit instead of his normal uniform of tattered jeans and T-shirt emblazoned with a *risqué* message that it was only the special appeal of his mother-in-law ('Pull yourself together, you lout') that had enabled him to carry on.

At this point in the service the vicar was asking the assembled company if anyone knew any reason why the marriage shouldn't go ahead. Nobody said anything, of course, but my informant said, well, they wouldn't, would they, not in church, but just wait till people got talking at the reception. That's where you heard the interesting titbits.

The next hymn was quite unknown to me. Apparently the vicar, who had written it, generally managed to sneak it into every marriage service he conducted. It was something to do with turning the world into a gigantic community centre. The vicar had not got round to composing a tune for it, so the organist had married it to a well-known tune from *Hymns Ancient and Modern* – a device that more or less worked if you repeated the last line of each verse.

The choir's final musical contribution was Bach's 'Jesu, joy of man's desiring'. My temporary colleague said this was a good potboiler for weddings, although the choir had never really got the hang of it. But it didn't matter much because it was always sung during the period in the service when, the bride and groom and their immediate attendants being temporarily out of sight in the vestry signing the register, the rest of the congregation amused themselves trying to spot members of the family who they'd been avoiding since Granddad's funeral two years ago, and no one would have noticed if the choir were standing on their heads singing 'Any old iron'.

Perhaps this wedding party were particularly anxious to get away to the reception. The organist played them out with his almost obligatory double version of the Grand March from 'Aida' but 'Moonlight and roses' wasn't needed this time. In a final chat he warmly invited me to drop in at 'the opera house' whenever I was around. I'd be particularly welcome at Sunday matins, he said, to help the choir keep the vicar in check. The vicar always tried to gabble through the canticles and psalms at twice the speed of everyone else, and often mucked up the whole show.

As I came out of the churchyard a little later, the last car carrying the residue of the wedding party was lurching away along the dirt road from the church and the choir members had long since disappeared by their secret ways. The great calm closed in again as the sleepy sounds of the insects in the tall grass reasserted themselves, and presently I became aware of another sound of contented peace. On a sun-warmed tombstone where I had paused, a large black cat sprawled, purring gently. Had I really just taken part in a big noisy wedding service in this secret place? Already I wondered. The cat looked up at me, then stretched luxuriously and closed his eyes.

12

Onward, Christian Soldier

There is always an awkward man on the church council who wants to get things done. He won't be content with 'looking into' a matter, or pondering it for two or three years. He demands that a concrete decision is reached there and then, and is therefore very unreasonable and annoying. He is not at all the right material for a church councillor and is really only someone who likes stirring up trouble.

In the country parish where a relation of mine is on the church council, they had a very fine example of this type of councillor. Within six months of his advent in the village – he had retired from the army forty years previously, and his face assumed a curious shade of purple if you didn't call him Major – he had got himself elected on to all the local committees and had formed three or four new ones, on to which he also got himself elected.

On the church council his enthusiasm knew no bounds and, at the very first meeting he attended, he insisted that the church should have a new heating system installed by the coming winter, and that an appeal should be launched immediately to furnish the necessary cash.

All the other members were dismayed and outraged. It was not as if they were unmindful of the need for a new heating system. For *years* the question had been on the agenda. They discussed it *very* fully all through the winter, by which time it was summer. The church was then quite warm enough and they shelved it till the next winter.

But now, before they knew what was happening, they had agreed to the Major's plans for an appeal, and a full programme of whist drives, garden fetes (if wet, in the Nag's Head's games-room), bingo sessions and choir concerts was soon in full swing. As far as any efforts by the choir were concerned, the general opinion seemed to be that it was bad enough having to put up with them every Sunday without enduring them through the week as well. But, on the whole, the congregation were a very loyal lot and felt that, after all, they were suffering in a good cause, so at each concert the village hall was packed to the doors and thunderous applause was dutifully given. (Only a few people were cowardly enough to send a donation and not turn up.)

And so efficiently and untiringly did the Major bully everyone, including the director of the heating firm, that, long before winter had set in, the new heating system was installed and ready for use.

The Sunday on which the heat was to be turned on for the first time at evensong was so fine that the sun shone swelteringly all day long. The spring and summer climate had, till then, been endearingly British. For weeks on end the television weathermen had taken a fiendish delight in pointing out on their maps large areas of hopeless weather which would grow even more hopeless. Even the Bank Holiday weekends had not been spared. Indeed, the church congregations at the Easter and Whitsun services had been the largest for a very long time. Then suddenly, on the Sunday of the new heating, even while the weathermen still gloated behind the protection of the television screens, the sun broke through.

It became so hot that the verger opened all the doors in the church, and every window that had not jammed solid through decades of disuse. He also resurrected a venerable electric fan which revolved very slowly, got very hot and filled the place with a smell of burning rubber.

But the Major had decreed that this was the day that the new heating should be demonstrated, and the congregation had to feel that they were getting value for their money, so the verger spent most of the day stoking the boiler to full capacity. He revelled in the way it devoured coke by the hundred-weight. He shovelled untiringly. He was a very good stoker and felt proud of his new boiler . . .

A good half-hour before evensong was due to commence most of the congregation had arrived and were standing about the church in groups, enthusiastically complaining about the colour and shape of the radiators, the rumoured cost of running them, and the curiously tropical heat. One of the choirboys was pointing out to a colleague that if you looked closely you could actually see the heatwaves rising round the pulpit. He said that when the vicar got up to preach, they would probably make his face go all funny, like when you looked into those distorting mirrors at the seaside. A tall, stooping gentleman, who was the church treasurer, looked around gloomily and mopped his brow. As he walked up the aisle to give a collection plate to another tall, stooping gentleman, who was removing a large woollen scarf which he always wore in church, he noticed from a hymn-board that the choir were doing an anthem that evening and this made him even more gloomy.

And then, just before the start of the service, the Major himself entered. He stood for a moment in the doorway, brisk, business-like, alert, sniffing approvingly at the heat. He bowed stiffly to those people who had not yet reached their seats and couldn't get out of his way. Then he clattered up to his front pew, by which stood the biggest radiator in the church. He patted it, stood back and admired it, and stood back a little further as it suddenly gurgled and appeared to shake itself. But it seemed quite friendly, and the Major proudly took up his position next to it, and fixed his eagle eyes on the door under the organ whence would soon emerge the choir.

The choir were the next item on the Major's list of urgent improvements, and he was observing them closely. He complained about them regularly every Sunday to the vicar, who passed the complaints to the organist, who took no notice whatsoever. The Major's point was that the choir did nothing but bawl their heads off, and the organist's point was that he'd known that for years, and if the Major thought he was going to mess about with *his* choir he had another thing coming.

It seemed that nothing – not even the overwhelming efforts of the new heating system – could

stop the choir bawling their heads off. By the end
of the service the Major had completely forgotten
the heating. That was a victory won, a triumph in
the past. One could not rest on past achievements.
One must now go ahead and tackle the choir –
immediately! He wiped the perspiration from his
face. Ignorance and slovenliness must not be toler-
ated. Choirmen who couldn't read a note of music

and refused to learn new hymn-tunes, and choir-boys who wore collars with bows under one ear, and filthy white plimsolls, must be rooted out. At the very next meeting of the church council he would suggest ... urge ... *demand* ... ! The congregation staggered, bemused, from the Turkish bath atmosphere into the comparative coolness of the churchyard. One member, who was a solid fuel merchant, was shaking his head confiding to a friend. 'The trouble *is* the coke situation, Horace,' he was explaining. 'This is a very *bad* area for coke. They'll *never* get enough for the winter. There's just *nothing* they can do about it.' But the Major would, and probably did, tell them differently. One had to suggest ... urge ... *demand* ... !

13

They Love Us Really

'I must report an unbelievable story,' bellowed my friend Teddy over the phone. 'Things are going berserk here in the village – absolutely berserk! It's all to do with this new lady curate who descended on us a few weeks ago – the vicar's carrying on at the other church and she's in charge of us. Well, she's got this sort of huge charisma and whenever she preaches on Sundays our usual congregation is swollen to bursting point by that crowd who we normally only see in church at Christmas and weddings and funerals. She always says the most outrageous things about the Church being completely out of touch and lazy and arrogant and failing miserably all over the place. And everyone gets indignant and furious with her and more and more people turn up at church each week to hear what awful things she'll dare say next.'

'Doesn't she *care* that everyone is indignant and furious with her?' I asked.

'She loves it,' said Teddy. 'She says she's making people think instead of blindly accepting threadbare dogma.'

'Would you say she's pretty thick-skinned?' I suggested.

'Well, actually she is rather pretty,' admitted Teddy. 'Anyway, at the end of the service where she has preached, a lot of the congregation lie in wait for her at the back of the church, all fuming and ready to "get" her – and then she flounces down to them, all smiles and full of this charisma thing and the next thing you know everyone is smiling too and nodding and agreeing with her and thanking her for such a thought-provoking sermon – and they all go home happy until the next sermon when they're all indignant and furious again.'

'So what does the Parochial Church Council think about all this?' I asked.

'Well, of course, they're indignant and furious all the time,' explained Teddy. 'Things are getting so upsetting with them they've had six emergency meetings during the last two months.'

I remembered Teddy's reports of previous PCC meetings in the serenity of the eighteenth-century thatched-roofed church hall where no one ever spoke an abrasive word and everyone always agreed with everyone else and carried on precisely as usual.

'So what are the PCC going to do?' I asked Teddy.

'Well, they're not used to people getting up and preaching such outlandish sermons,' he sympathized. 'They just keep on meeting and fixing the date of the *next* meeting and getting more and more upset.'

'And what about the choir?' I asked, intrigued. 'Do they also get indignant and furious over the lady's sermons? What do you think?'

'Think? Oh, nothing really,' Teddy said comfortably. 'The choir never listen to sermons. It's a sort of tradition – they do crosswords or go to sleep. They couldn't hear much anyway, up there in the choirstalls behind the chancel screen – it's out of the way and nice and quiet – unless, of course, we get one of those visiting preachers who shout and rave and keep on banging on the pulpit. But we don't get many of them these days.'

Some weeks later I was in Teddy's delightful village on one of my periodic visits, which always include joining the choir for the Sunday services. In the vestry before choral matins members of the choir were unhurriedly searching for their cassocks and surplices. Members of the choir at Teddy's church are always unhurriedly searching for their cassocks and surplices before matins. This is because of the enthusiastic action of a terrifyingly active young woman, only ever referred to as 'the general's daughter', who has a fixation about the choir appearing immaculately turned out on all occasions. During the week she collects their robes from the choir vestry and washes and irons everything she can lay her hands on. Then she brings them back to the vestry and hangs them neatly and tidily in all the wrong places. Thus the traditional pre-matins search!

Teddy, being a sidesman and not a choir member, didn't have to go through the searching routine but from some mysterious source of his own, safe from the attentions of the general's daughter, he produced a cassock and surplice for me and went off to his duty of ushering in the enlarged congregation. A few minutes later the new lady curate herself made her entry into the choir vestry. She looked very young and had truly beautiful fair hair in three shimmering shades that swung free to the middle of her back. She wore a stylish dark blue gown, gold embroidered slippers and the famous charismatic smile.

No one took any notice of her. Everyone was still too engrossed detecting the whereabouts of their robes. She moved slowly around the walls studying the large sepia photographs of past organists and choir members who glared in all directions. The charismatic smile slowly faded into an expression, I thought, of puzzlement. As she came near to me the smile returned with full vigour. 'I wonder why they never *smiled* in these photographs,' she said. 'These people all look so strait-laced.'

'People were not supposed to smile in Victorian photos,' I said. 'It wasn't done.'

She indicated the figure in a photograph nearest to us, of what looked like a Victorian dandy. 'But just look at *him*! I wonder why he looked so grim,' she pondered.

'He,' came the gravelly voice of a very large choirman at her shoulder, 'was my great-grandfather – organist here for fifty years. When you have to deal with the clergy for fifty years you do tend to get grim.'

The glamorous New Age cleric held her smile admirably. 'Fifty years! What a wonderful record!' she enthused.

'We've only had three organists here in a century,' continued the gravel-voiced one, 'my great-grandfather, my grandfather and my father Sid.' Everyone knew Sid the present organist, of course, he had already served sixty years in the post, a splendid octogenarian dandy who was never without his buttonhole and still wore spats on Sunday and whose photograph, the last on the wall, was almost indistinguishable from that of his forebear who we'd been discussing.

At this juncture the said Sid arrived in all his Victorian elegance, his glory only slightly dimmed by the sight of immaculate black trousers anchored above spotless spats and gleaming shoes by pillar-box-red cycle clips. Sid was an ardent cyclist. Immediately he started passing out the music for the morning's service, battered, limp-with-use copies, liberally damp-spotted which had doubtless been handed out in the same manner a century ago by Sid's forebear.

'Sid,' complained a small round choirboy examining his antique copy, 'mine's got a hole in it. I can't read the music.'

An attractive choirgirl with hair that rivalled the new lady curate's but was pinioned with a huge yellow sparkling bow, making her appear like a cigarette and chocolate salesgirl in a pre-war super cinema, glanced at the boy's music and regarded him with disdain. 'It's all right, Sir,' she assured Sid, 'he doesn't know what he's talking about – the hole is in the *bass* line. The treble line is perfectly all right.'

A few minutes later we all lined up behind the large gravel-voiced choirman who also acted as crucifer, and having uttered his usual unprintable threats to the two leading choirboys on what would happen to them if they tried to get in front of him during the procession into the chancel, 'making the whole show look like a three-horse race', the new lady curate bounced forward beaming. 'Hi, choir!' she greeted them. 'It's your special day! I'm going to preach on church music and church choirs.'

'Now what does she mean? What's she up to now?' asked the man next to me who was wrestling violently with the cellophane wrapper of a packet of throat lozenges.

'The sermon's going to be about us,' I said, but I don't think he heard me because at that moment his packet of lozenges burst, scattering its contents far and wide over the floor. While he and half the rest of the choir started retrieving the lozenges and dusting off each one carefully ('These are very expensive y'know,') everyone else broke ranks and a choirgirl, the one with the big yellow bow who had taken out a mirror and was closely studying the shape of her eyebrows, remarked to all and sundry, 'What does she want to talk about us for? I should think there's enough gossip about us already. There always is – people complaining about our Sunday papers left in the choirstalls, people saying we talk too loudly in the quiet bits of the service, people going on and on about the noise in the Goat and Compasses after choir practice on Friday nights, people saying we haven't a clue how to sing.'

'Well, the lady's a New Age priest,' I said, 'she's keen, forward looking. I expect she wants to update the choir – and Sid.'

'Update Sid?' she uttered incredulously. 'How can you update Sid? Sid wouldn't be Sid if you updated him – and we do what Sid wants, so anyone who thinks they can update the choir is living in the realms of fantasy.'

'Ah, don't worry,' soothed a plump little tenor. 'The congregation have *always* complained about the choir. It's a revered tradition – an attitude of affection. They love us really – love us as we are. They're proud of us up there in the choirstalls. We're the smartest robed choir for miles, a credit to the church! And look at Sid – a veritable fashion icon. Why do you think they all insist on having the choir at their weddings? They love us!'

Eventually, a choirboy who had crawled round the vestry three times and thereby covered his cassock with dust and candle droppings announced that he'd found the final lozenge and we all re-assembled behind Gravel Voice. Throughout the entire interval the lady curate had held firmly to her charismatic smile. 'Good, splendid!' she beamed and we all moved in a dignified shuffle into the chancel, fifteen minutes late, while a number of important looking members of the congregation pointedly consulted their watches.

True to tradition, the choir didn't listen to a word of the sermon and true to form most of the congregation massed at the back of the church after the service to barrack the preacher furiously. And true to tradition also, most of the congregation continued to talk about the choir's behavioural shortcomings and the alleged fact that they haven't a clue how to sing.

And no one at all would dream of church life without the familiar changeless presence of Sid's choir or for that matter now, the new lady curate and her 'all change' sermons. It's a lovely, lively place, my friend Teddy's parish and all is well.

What a splendid institution is the Church of England! May it never *really* change.

14

The Poachers

At the picture-postcard village church (partly thatched, partly falling down) where my friend Oscar is a long-term chorister, relations between the vicar and the choir couldn't be more harmonious. The vicar never interferes with the music, leaving the choice of hymns and settings for the services entirely to the choir who leave it entirely to the organist who sticks faithfully to a list handed down from the last organist but one. The choir and organist greatly appreciate the vicar's attitude and, in return, always keep the sound of their homely chatter during the sermon down to a reasonable hum, and immediately and wholeheartedly respond to the vicar's well-known winter appeals for volunteers to coax the church's historic heating system back to life and to help protect the village hall during the nightmare of the Sunday School Christmas party.

Indeed, the annual Sunday School party is very

much welcomed by senior members of the choir as a great opportunity to do some profitable poaching. In order that the congregation may get a little peace and quiet and have a chance of hearing what the vicar is talking about at Sunday morning service, the children of this parish are, from a very early, post-creche, age, drafted into the Sunday School into the all-embracing care of a lovely spirited lady who still believes firmly that all children are at heart the angelic beings of Victorian children's hymns. With a clear and pure conscience she dismisses all junior vandalism and violence as merely the result of appealing high spirits. Among those pupils with the most appealing high spirits are always a clutch of potential choir recruits and regularly each year, while policing the Sunday School Christmas party, the senior choir members seek to entice specially targeted ones away from the Sunday School and into the (paid) treble section of the choir. The ploy works well. The lovely spirited lady looks upon the enticement as a richly deserved reward for her angelic charges and indeed a step up the ladder of sainthood, and the budding saints like the idea too, particularly the bit about being paid to come to church.

Of course, once in the choir, they soon have to

come to terms with the fact that the organist is quite unlike the lovely spirited lady and considers them all as over-indulged hooligans who are a necessary evil in the maintaining of a traditional church choir, the necessary evil being kept within decent bounds by the imposition of large fines for misconduct (musical and otherwise) which can seriously deplete and sometimes be found to have completely exhausted the whole amount of one's pay when pay day comes round.

I am a guest in the choir once a year on horse-show Sunday. The one surface-rippling event in the serene pool of village life (apart from the Sunday School party) is without doubt the summer horse show. It doesn't feature in any important national show calendars and is concerned entirely with cart-horses, but over the years its popularity over a considerable surrounding area has grown amazingly. True to tradition, as the carthorse all but disappeared from our streets and fields, the general public suddenly realized how much they admired, and were fascinated by, those splendid beasts, and more and more spectators poured into the village each year on horse-show Sunday. As horse numbers continued to decline, spectator numbers rose. Some years ago when around 5,000 people turned up to see thirty horses, Oscar, who is on the horse-show committee, forecast that in another five years there would be 10,000 people looking at fifteen horses and eventually they would have 100,000 people watching a single horse.

Happily, as the big horses made a dramatic comeback in promotional and leisure fields, Oscar's prophecy proved wrong and the show now goes from strength to strength. Oscar always arranges for the full participation of the church choir in the show and we sing drinking songs on a brewery dray and in the beer tent after matins. Then, after the close of the show, there is a special festal evensong when a procession of drays brings people to church where we all sing 'All things bright and beautiful' and 'Fight the good fight' and everybody is jolly and gives lots of spare change to the organ fund.

On the latest occasion of the summer horse show, however, the vicar made an unprecedented request to the organist at very short notice. He would be most grateful if – just for this year – it would be possible to substitute a new hymn for 'Fight the good fight'. He explained that the hymn in question was the absolute favourite of an elder sister of his who lived in Canada and would be making her first visit to see him in over forty years, and was keen to attend the horse-show evensong. He fully realized that normally the hymns for this service, like all others, were strictly those on the handed-down list from the last organist but one, but in the circumstances perhaps – in view of the very special circumstances . . .

In the vestry just before the service the organist, a tall, neat, nattily dressed man with a knowing, crinkled face, gathered the choir around him. 'He wants us to sing this new thing for his sister,' he explained, handing out the music copies the vicar had supplied. 'As you can see, it's one of those "Clap hands, here comes Charlie" efforts, photocopied on a bit of paper with no author and no composer – and no wonder – where you have to sing two lines three times and then shout "Alleluia" or "Hurray" or something.'

One of our basses was regarding his hymn-sheet with a baffled expression. 'That's the trouble, of course,' he rumbled. 'That's the real trouble. When you've got a man like our *last* vicar – always sticking his nose in and trying to change everything – it's a pleasure to tell him what he can do with his ideas. But when you've got a bloke like *this* one – never interferes and always ready to stand you a pint – you can't really say no.'

So we didn't say no, and even the bass spokesman thundered out the vicar's sister's favourite hymn as if he'd known and loved it from the cradle. Only his nearest colleagues heard him exclaim, as the last jolly shout echoed round the church, 'Where do they dig up this rubbish?' So the vicar's sister's ecstasy on hearing her favourite 'praise song' sung in 'such a thrilling, uplifting way' was not spoiled.

After the service most of the choir and congregation moved across the road to the large field where the horse show had been held and watched huge Shire horses being fed and watered and loaded into horse-boxes. The lovely spirited Sunday School lady was there too, beaming proudly at her swarming pupils who were all exhibiting their appealing high spirits by pursuing each other between the horses' legs and examining the outsized hooves at close quarters. 'Such good-tempered horses, Shires,' remarked the organist at my elbow. 'Still,' he added hopefully, 'perhaps one of them will get fed up in a minute and kick out.'

He raised his voice to choir-practice pitch. 'Get away from those hooves!' His roar echoed round the field. The Shires stood unperturbed. The budding saints scattered. The organist smiled in grim anticipation. 'I'll have most of 'em in the choir next year,' he gloated.

'Well, if you can get them up to the standard of your present trebles that will be marvellous,' I assured him. 'I thought their singing was absolutely splendid today.'

'It's amazing what you can do with a bunch of hooligans if you show them who's master,' he agreed. 'It's the same with the vicar.'

'But the vicar's not a hooligan, surely?' I exclaimed, slightly shocked. 'He always seems so polite and considerate.'

'Maybe, but we still have to keep a sharp eye on him,' he warned. 'You see, now we've given in to him about singing his sister's hymn he'll be encouraged to start pushing other things on to us as well. I know he's got a whole book of those funny sort of new hymns. He'd love to sing some of *those* at matins.'

'But he can't sing,' I said.

'He thinks he can,' said the organist. 'When he first came here I had no end of a job convincing him that we all felt that someone in the choir should sing the versicles for him because we were anxious that he should save his voice for the sermon. He seemed very suspicious, I can tell you.'

A big bouncy choirgirl who always sang with the utmost healthy vigour no matter what marks of expression the composer had indicated came up to us, leading her father's Shire horse. She pointed to her huge charge's red rosette. 'A second last year, a first this year. How about that!' she beamed. Being equally captivated, as she obviously was, with the charms of Shire horses, I found myself quite naturally talking to this one and congratulating him on his win while she told him we thought he was a very handsome clever boy. And there we stood chatting – although the horse couldn't really get a word in edgeways – until the organist tapped the choirgirl on the shoulder in a businesslike way and said he hoped she'd got her solo ready for next Sunday's anthem because he didn't expect to be mucking about drumming it into her at the last minute before the service. She said she knew her solo backwards and the organist said that probably was just about how she *did* know it, and she insisted that he pat her horse to show how pleased he was that he'd won a first. A delightful pair, they meandered away across the field. The organist stood watching. 'Of course, we have *them* in the choir now,' he remarked meditatively.

'Who?' I asked. 'Shire horses?'

'Young women,' he said. 'In my younger days we only had choirboys. Now it's choirgirls. We've got more girls than boys now.'

'Things change,' I said.

His voice became warm and comfortable. 'Not really,' he said. 'They're all hooligans. Nothing changes. No, nothing really changes, thank goodness. We're lucky with our choir.'

15

The Spearhead

A fellow chorister and office colleague of mine retired a year or two ago and promptly escaped from the City and disappeared into the remoteness of remotest East Anglia with his wife and three cats where he immediately joined the village church choir and began to enjoy himself immensely. We've kept in touch and occasionally I too escape from the City and stay with them and help out in the choir. George always has a good story to tell. He had one now.

'The man's a positive menace,' fumed George. He spoke of the new organist who had lately descended on the village church. Since the revered bachelor octogenarian organist who had been in charge of the choir for over fifty years had suddenly fallen in love, got married and gone to live in Spain, the parish had been waiting for a replacement when suddenly, as if by magic, the new man appeared from goodness knows where and offered to take over the choir 'as a Christian labour of love' without requiring even payment of expenses. Whereupon the vicar and the parochial church council enthusiastically decided that here was exactly the kind of dedicated musician they wanted and impressed on the choir how lucky they (the choir) were going to be.

The new man, another bachelor, but perhaps a half a century younger than his predecessor, lost no time in announcing in the parish magazine that he had a thrilling vision of the choir being transformed by unquestioning dedication and constant hard work into nothing less than the spearhead of a glorious revival of great choral singing in that part of the country.

'Did he ask the choir if they *wanted* to be the spearhead of a glorious revival?' I enquired. 'I mean, you lot just like belting out hymns at matins on Sunday and having a quick-run through of a tune or two on Friday nights before adjourning to the Dog and Duck.'

'No, he didn't ask us,' said George, 'he *told* us! A positive menace!'

'Mind you,' I told him, 'most new organists carry on like that when they first appear; they try to impress. I wouldn't worry too much – they calm down in time.'

George appeared less than convinced. 'This one won't,' he asserted. 'He's got this vision, y'see. He's already called three special choir meetings to explain it – it all sounds like a nightmare.'

We were reclining, George and I, on this warm still, summer Sunday afternoon, around the doorway of George's potting shed at the bottom of his long, narrow, meandering back garden. A pleasant, peaceful haven this, quite hidden from his cottage by high screens of runner beans, great clumps of hollyhocks and giant sunflowers and two ancient apple trees. This was George's secret domain to where he retreated during the frequent invasions of the cottage by his wife's numerous committees who dealt with everything in the village from church cleaning and flower arranging to poetry readings, protests about rubbish collection, non-operating streetlamps and people waiting for the twice-a-week bus that had a habit of turning up once a week.

'I still say you needn't worry too much about this organist character,' I persisted. 'He'll change his ideas, you'll see. Your wife will doubtless set up one of her committees and tell him . . .'

'Tell him!' exploded George. 'Just wait till you meet him. He's built like a retired heavyweight boxer and has a voice like a demented foghorn. In the coffee room after Sunday morning service he blunders all over the place gripping people's hands and slapping them on the back – even tiny old ladies – and butts in on everybody's conversations and says they're going to have a real, top-rate, superb choir up in the choirstalls in the next few months and people will be coming to our church from all over the place to hear us.'

'Oh,' I said.

George sighed gustily. 'He says the time is ripe for strong, fearless leadership in the choir, unswerving commitment, less arguing, less opposition to vital views.'

'He *actually said* all that?' I asked.

'Well, they're my words,' confessed George. 'He put it a lot more forcefully and convincingly, of course. In his last parish he was a leading light in the local amateur dramatic society.'

'I think I've got the picture,' I said.

'He's got a cat who's just like him,' continued George, 'a great big, battle-scarred ginger tom called Fred who goes around beating up all the other cats in the neighbourhood who get in his way.'

'A redeeming feature!' I exclaimed. 'The man can't be all that bad if he likes cats.'

'Well, no, he's not really, I suppose,' agreed

George. 'It's just that he's got this *vision*. It's always difficult dealing with organists who have got visions. Y'see, he's not content just playing through the services on Sundays and keeping the choirgirls in order. He's always on about this spearhead thing and keeps on calling extra rehearsals and going on and on about standing and breathing properly and not taking our eyes off him when he's conducting.' He frowned darkly. 'He's pushing his luck just a little too far.'

Later that afternoon we made our way to the church for evensong and, avoiding the inevitable congestion in the narrow main entrance – the vicar was one of those who went in for a rumbustious congregational handshaking and chattering routine *before* the service as well as afterwards – we went the way of the knowledgeable few of the congregation who, not being really ready for such a rowdy show of Christian fellowship on a nice quiet Sunday evening, made their way into church through a sort of secret doorway at the back of the chancel which was cosily hidden behind a battery of dustbins full of dead flowers, and a pile of broken gravestones including headless, limbless cherubs used as a support for the oldest choirman's veteran bike.

In the choir vestry four or five small choirboys

were gathered around a battered piano (all choir vestry pianos seem to be battered) where the new organist was endeavouring to get one of them to sing the first verse of 'Hark, my Soul, it is the Lord'. The boy in question was making what the organist called 'a most unholy sound, an insult to the Deity' each time he attempted to sing. In fact, each time the sound became more unholy and more insulting until, abandoning any further musical instruction, the organist raised his eyes to heaven and intoned with barely controlled intensity, 'Unless you cease lolling all over the piano and sing the verse so that I can vaguely recognize it, you will leave the choir forthwith and, of course, *the choir football team as well.*' Whereupon the boy assumed an expression of angelic purity and sang the verse in a voice of truly touching beauty.

The organist rose, scattering the boys from his presence like annoying crumbs from his lap. George introduced me and he greeted me with a crushing handshake and Olympian smile. 'A visitor, eh?' he loomed. 'We don't have auditions for visitors – yet. There will be auditions for the whole choir soon. We must sort out what kind of talent we have here.'

He released my numbed hand and George moved me across to the robes cupboard to find me a spare cassock and surplice among a very sorry collection that looked as though they should have been pensioned off at least half a century ago. He was grinning wickedly. 'The future looks intriguing,' he whispered. 'I can hardly wait for the sorting out of our talent! Auditions! Nearly all the talent we have here is the same as we had forty years ago only a bit more rusty now. We *have* got some young girl sopranos, but their main talent is in their good looks. The vicar does like to see a young attractive front row in the choir. None of them can read music or anything like that of course but they do make for a cheery atmosphere for the congregation. Auditions! This is going to be just wonderful!'

Five or six of the long-time tenor and bass talent had now arrived and were growling together in a corner, and members of the vicar's attractive front row were carefully arranging their appearances before the spotty vestry mirror. A few minutes later, having completed his big joyful congregational welcome routine, the vicar, a young eager looking man with a shock of red hair, scuttled into the vestry and started another joyful welcome for the choir, the later strains of which were drowned out by gigantic opening chords from the organ signalling the commencement of the service. The choir processed into the chancel at a smart shuffle led by the crucifer, a veteran military-looking type who warned the leading choirboys to 'keep behind me, not up level with me or it looks like a three horse race to the altar'.

Being an alto I found myself seated next to Madge, a statuesque lady of formidable mien who lived next door to the church and bred ton-weight champion Suffolk Punch horses and took no nonsense from anyone. She was the choir's only contralto. Her voice nevertheless was quite effective enough to cope easily with the rest of the choir (some people said it was *more* than enough). Her male family forebears had been mixed up in all the wars and most of the military skirmishes through-out the eighteenth and nineteenth centuries and their memorial stained-glass windows and promi-nent plaques commanded attention everywhere in the church, and their tombs dominated the church-yard just as today Madge dominated the choir.

As the service progressed I became increasingly aware of her disapproving, indeed shocked, eyes boring into me. When we sat for the sermon she moved threateningly close to me. '*Where* did you dig up that disgusting outfit?' she hissed. 'The sur-plice is absolutely *filthy* and the cassock looks like a thoroughly disreputable version of something my great grandfather is wearing in the 1870 photo of the choir that's in the vestry!' Her look of horror intensified. 'It probably is the original one!'

A mischievous spirit was upon me. 'Certainly your new organist won't tolerate choir members wearing things like these that I'm wearing for much longer,' I affirmed. 'They are even worse than those you and the rest of the choir have got. When he transforms you all into that spearhead of a glorious revival of great choral singing there is no way you'll be allowed to appear at top musical festivals on the television wearing things like this.'

'An interesting young man, our new organist,' she mused. 'So enthusiastic, so endearingly optimistic – so naïve. I shall certainly back him to the hilt – not in his fantasy of our choir becoming synonymous with anything to do with good singing, of course – did you ever hear such nonsense – but one must respect and support and encourage those with vision and initiative. You never know, the new man might prevail on the Church Council to pay for a set of new choir robes and if he eventually inveigles one or two of the wearers to master the knack of reading music, that will be a bonus indeed, will it not?'

I heard from George recently. The choir have got their new robes and the vicar is so impressed with the new organist's almost daily flow of thinking new ideas for the future of the choir that he's bestowed on him the official title of 'Parish Director of Music'.

Nevertheless as far as George knows, there's still no one in the front row who can read music and the organist, with the irresistible encouragement of Madge the formidable, is showing definite signs of enjoying the choir's traditional Friday night 'quick run through' practices which end up in the Dog and Duck and has not mentioned auditions for quite a while. Rome wasn't built in a day, so meanwhile everything is carrying on precisely and as happily as ever and, as George says, who can ask for more than that?

16

Charlie Robinson

In the Hampshire village where I sometimes spend a few days, the church choir has a quaint and revered tradition. Forty years ago the vestry was redecorated, and while the work was in progress the choir was obliged to find alternative accommodation for Friday night choir practice. The then vicar had kindly offered the use of his conservatory. The place was not ideal as it was full of dust-laden aspidistras, broken flowerpots, and a retired mangle. Moreover, it was necessary to trundle the church piano back and forth, from the vestry to the conservatory, right across the vicar's lawn.

But despite these drawbacks the choir soon became so happily attached to the conservatory that, when the vestry was reopened, they were in no great hurry to return. In fact, they never hurried at all and, today, the tradition of Friday night practice in the vicar's conservatory is so strong, and the ruts marking the passage of the piano across the vicar's lawn so permanent, that I doubt if practice will *ever* be held anywhere else.

Of course, over the years the place has become even more crowded. The plants have flourished exceedingly and are now capable of supporting a much wider area of dust, and the mangle has been joined by a cracked copper, which looks quite at home in the mountain of broken flowerpots. But there is still room for the three-legged chairs and backless garden seats which accommodate the choir, so everything carries on most pleasantly.

One wet summer evening I was waiting in the vicarage to attend a practice, and the vicar's wife had thoughtfully handed me a cup of that tea which always appears to be brewing by the gallon in English vicarages. Both being fanatical cat-lovers, the conversation turned naturally on the vicarage cat. He was a monstrous tabby affair who had never joined a fight in his life, but managed to keep at bay every other cat for miles, by uttering the most blood-curdling noises from the top of the Manor House mausoleum.

His favourite pastime was getting lost in the organ just before a service was due to begin. He would sit wailing in the middle of a forest of organ pipes until the organist, in a frantic effort to rescue him, was well covered with dirt and cobwebs, and would then escape quite easily by an exit known only to himself. The vicar's wife said he was called Charlie Robinson, for the simple reason that he *looked* like Charlie Robinson. Charlie himself (the cat) appeared to disagree with this, however, because he only ever answered to the name of Pudden.

At this point a loud grinding sound, reminiscent of a veteran tram turning into the depot, heralded the arrival of the piano in the conservatory. Simultaneously, choir members began to appear from all directions. Some came in at the ever open vicarage front door, neatly overstepping the mat with one stride and strewing an even layer of wet gravel all over the polished floor; two or three entered through the french windows via the vicar's favourite flowerbed; and one man came up from the basement kitchen carrying a large steaming saucepan from which issued the most evil odour. On his way up, he explained to the vicar's wife that he had noticed that Charlie Robinson's fish had boiled dry, and should he put it out on the lawn till the smell died down . . . ?

Everything seemed very leisurely. For a while the gentlemen of the choir talked and filled the sitting-room with large clouds of smoke. But they had to *stand* around, because there was no room on the overcrowded arms of the vicar's best chairs. Then, with the arrival of the organist, we drifted into the conservatory.

We all liked the organist. He was a tall, stooping middle-aged bachelor, and he never seemed to lose his temper with us. If, during the rehearsal of an anthem, the basses were making a more excruciating row than usual, he never showed them up, but merely whispered good naturedly, 'You'd better just *hum* that bit.' He never whispered anything to me, because I was the only male alto, and was also effectively drowned by a large bellowing lady, who had sung contralto in the choir from pre-conservatory days and who never took any notice of organists whether they whispered or raved.

Having balanced ourselves on the rickety chairs and garden seats, the organist announced that we'd 'run through the hymns for Sunday'. This consisted primarily of the organist thumping out the tune on the tram-like piano before you could even find the place and, just as you found it, exclaiming, 'Well, I think we know *that* one all right', and going on to the next. You could never really catch up with him, but the procedure did keep you alert and stopped your interest from wandering.

We now moved to the psalms. These went very well on the whole. We couldn't hear much of the sopranos for the first few verses, but that was quite understandable since Charlie Robinson, who always liked to look in on choir practice, had arrived, only this time carrying a large bitterly complaining rat.

An interesting scuffle took place among the ladies' feet, and this momentarily threatened to upset the whole balance of the choir, but the rat finally made his point and escaped. And by the time we'd reached verse seven the soprano line was quite restored.

We now came to the highlight of the practice – the anthem. And how we enjoyed that! It was one of those delightfully treacly Victorian compositions which I, in my ignorance, shall always love. It started off with a rousing chorus followed by a quartet which reminded me of those singing waiters in the hey-day of the music hall. Then a very fruity tenor, singing a recitative lifted wholesale from Italian romantic opera, led us to the final chorus. This was so enthusiastically tackled that we got a little out of hand. The organist didn't believe in conducting: whenever we galloped, or dragged, or

just broke down, a few sharp slaps on the mangle with a handy plant cane always put things right. And on this occasion we finished the practice more or less together with the happy feeling of a job well done.

I helped the organist and the fruity tenor to move the piano back across the lawn to the vestry. As it fell back against the wall, a heart-rending wail came from the heart of the organ. The organist was all concern. 'Charlie Robinson's got himself lost in the organ again,' he explained, and removing a panel, plunged into the darkness under the bellows.

Five minutes later when he must have been well on his way to the top of the organ, Charlie Robinson appeared, calmly walking across the vestry. 'Charlie Robinson!' I remonstrated. 'Pudden!' At this he stopped, and looked back over his shoulder. And then, I'm sure, he winked.

17

Grumbling is Good for You

It is a regrettable fact that in some parishes the presence of the church choir is, for the most part, ignored. The choir have always been there, like the bad stained-glass windows and the damp-stained patches on the west wall, and the congregation have long since ceased giving them any thought or consideration. The position is very different in a certain village church where my friend Felix (his father was a fanatical admirer of Mendelssohn and his mother was an early fan of the famous cartoon cat) is organist and choirmaster. There the choir are always in the thoughts of the congregation. They keep thinking what a relief it will be when the bass with a voice like an enraged football hooligan eventually decides to retire, and they constantly consider with desperate hope the possibility of two or three of the choirgirls getting married and raising families and not having time on Sundays to shriek through the hymns and psalms half a bar ahead of the organ and the rest of the choir.

The vicar is aware of the feelings of the congregation but he also possesses a voice like unto that of an enraged football hooligan and, further, he thinks the church is very lucky in having such attractive, keen choirgirls. In fact he is only too eager to inform all who mention the choir to him – and some of those who find it unmentionable as well – that he revels in a jolly good uninhibited sing, and if there's one thing the choir are good at it's uninhibited singing.

Felix is a fervent lover of tradition. One of his best loved and immovable traditions is that of choir practice. It takes place every Sunday morning about half an hour before matins is due to start. As soon as a few early stragglers turn up, Felix gathers them around the vestry piano and they start to run through the music for the service. The small band dispose of the psalms and canticles in something under five minutes – Felix thumps out the chants one after the other in a sort of continuous medley and choir members nod their heads and say they know them all, and that leaves Felix free to concentrate wholly on the favourites, the hymns. All these are also well known, being always chosen from a small collection of warlike Victorian hymns with appropriately militaristic tunes that are used throughout the year whatever the season. Nevertheless, every verse of every hymn is sung at the practice in order to warm up for the service, and as more and more choir members arrive the racket grows louder and louder until just before matins it threatens to drown out the sound of the bells, which generally set up some splendid competition as the volume of sound from the choir grows more belligerent. The bellringers always have the final advantage, however, because they carry on after the choir have to stop in order to line up and shuffle into the chancel to start the service.

As will be realized, there is no provision for a 'quiet time' for the congregation before the service, but the vicar does compensate for this by having what he calls 'meditative silence' at the commencement of the service. This gives the choir breathing space to cough, drop books, and generally settle themselves into the choirstalls, and time for the latecomers in the congregation to clatter through the squeaking doors and greet each other in the jolly manner of customers arriving in the pub for a convivial get-together. The bellringers, having completed their duty, can also be heard clumping down the three dozen hollow stairs from the belfry, discussing what went wrong with the peal.

I am always made very welcome in the choir when I visit Felix, and the most recent occasion was on a scorching hot Sunday morning in August. As we processed back into the vestry after the service, brilliant golden sunlight was streaming through the open doorway and lightening up the dust-laden dark varnished cupboards and the faded photographs of old vicars and Victorian choir outings that lined the grey stone walls. The church is early Victorian and, I believe, a listed building. Jutting from a corner of the vestry is one of those wide oblong yellow sinks that is so shallow that it encourages water to splash all over the place as soon as you turn the tap on more than a second or two – and this one is supplied by the heftiest brass tap I've ever seen that responds only to the most violent force and retaliates by thoroughly drenching the forcer. I think the combination must be listed along with the church. Anyway, it held an urgent attraction for the men of the choir on this sweltering summer morning. Their substantial crimson cassocks were discarded almost before vestry dismissal prayer was said, ties were removed and the water cascaded all over the historic threadbare carpet well beyond the boundaries of the yellow sink.

By contrast, the choirgirls stood around talking,

looking cool, unperturbed and very attractive in their crimson gowns and snow-white cravats. The men straggled out into the churchyard, dishevelled, red-faced and wet, and assuredly on their way to the One-Eyed Pheasant. Felix finished his voluntary – a favourite of mine that sounds as though it started life played on a steam roundabout organ – and came into the vestry with the vicar, who had finished shaking hands with the departing congregation and who now proceeded with his routine flattery of the girls about their delightful singing ('I was saying to my wife at dinner only last night how fortunate we are – how very fortunate . . .'). Then Felix led me off to lunch, and a choirgirl, a dark-haired charmer who lives next door to him, walked with us. In the churchyard some of the congregation lingered in small groups. A group of three middle-aged ladies of important appearance stood near the gate in loud conversation. '*They* want the choir to sing Vivaldi and that kind of thing,' informed the choirgirl in a conspiratorial whisper.

'What for?' asked Felix.

'They're always on about it to my mother at the WI,' enlarged the choirgirl. 'In fact, about half the congregation are – and the other half just complain that we make an awful noise.'

'There's no satisfying some people,' said Felix.

'They say that Vivaldi is uplifting and inspiring,' said the choirgirl.

'Don't they like what you sing?' I asked.

She opened her eyes wide at me and looked gorgeous. 'The one in the fur cape – in the middle of August, too! – says she goes home from church every Sunday with a raging headache because of us,' she said.

We drew abreast of the conferring ladies. Felix and I greeted them, and Fur Cape smiled at us as if from a great frosty height. 'How did you enjoy the singing this morning?' asked the choirgirl enthusiastically. 'Smashing, wasn't it – a real good bash, don't you think?'

The lady smiled at her as from an even greater frosty height and we bowed ourselves from the presence.

'Now you've done it,' admonished Felix. 'Now she won't make any more raspberry jam for the organ fund.'

But, of course, the lady *did* make more raspberry jam for the organ fund and tons of chutney too, and every jar was eagerly snapped up at the next organ fund sale. Indeed, as usual, the sale was a roaring success with nothing left on the stalls at the end of the day but a battered tin kettle, a wad of parish magazines, a lot of odd shoes and some unframed photographs of people's grandfathers in Boer War uniforms.

Immediately following the sale, the evening concluded with an old-time music hall concert put on by the choir to show their gratitude for the organ fund support, and all members of the congregation were invited. Of course, the inevitable rumours had reached Felix and members of the choir that some of the congregation were saying things like 'As if we don't have enough of them on Sunday without having to put up with them on Saturday as well' and 'Let's hope that the long-service bass doesn't sing "Boots" again this year. I got quite alarmed last time when he started turning purple in the last verse.'

But Felix's church is a truly united one, despite the lack of Vivaldi. On the night of the concert the village hall was crammed to the rafters. The bass did sing 'Boots' again, and this time also led the audience in rendering a roof-raising performance of 'Roll out the barrel'. And at the end of the evening the superior lady with the fur cape suddenly realized that she had not only joined in vigorously with 'Any old iron' but had bawled out 'More! More!' She felt ashamed and quite elated.

Felix's delightful choirgirl neighbour stood by
me on the stage watching the audience struggling
out through the exit lugging their bulging bags of
raspberry jam and chutney and manhandling the
useless junk they had purchased to donate them
back to the next organ fund sale. 'This'll keep them
happy for a bit,' she opined. 'They'll say nice things
to my mother about the choir for a week or two.

Then they'll start grousing again and saying they want Vivaldi and not so much noise. They always do.'

'Will it matter?' I asked.

She wrinkled her nose in a smile that was pure enchantment. I wondered if she would stay in the choir and grow old there, as so many of us do. 'Will it matter? No,' she said warmly. 'We *all* grumble. We *enjoy* grumbling. It keeps us happy, doesn't it?'

18

No Progress Report

A friend of mine who is organist and choirmaster of a particularly large, unmusical and unruly village church choir tries to create interest among the choirboys' parents by issuing quarterly reports on their sons' progress. He maintains that it's not possible to do anything with the adult members of the choir because they've been in the same bigoted rut for so long that they obviously haven't the slightest intention of ever learning any new music or, indeed, learning to sing the old music bearably. They won't even resign, or assist him in any way at all. They just keep coming to choir practices and carrying on as they've always carried on and always will carry on.

But my friend thinks that there is a faint hope for the boys, if only he can get the backing of the parents. Written reports on children invariably impress parents. They get extremely cross, of course, if the reports are unfavourable, and are inclined to write vitriolic letters or personally threaten the authority which issued the reports, but at least they show interest.

And this particular organist is very careful not to issue offensive reports. If a boy has a bad record for attendance or behaviour he always says so, but sweetens the pill by enthusing over some encouraging sign, real or imaginary, in his singing, or the fact that he can now read Roman numerals well enough to find the places in the psalms on his own.

On the other hand, if a boy has proved himself an utter incompetent and is thoroughly tuneless and senseless, he always writes, 'There is room for improvement, and I am sure this will come', and devoutly hopes that for some reason – any reason – the parents will take the boy away and plague some other choir with him.

I have sung in his choir on several occasions and am almost accepted as a native. It was not surprising, therefore, that I was hailed in a most friendly manner by half a dozen choirboys as I left the railway station on my arrival in the village for a recent weekend visit.

They were all perched tidily on an ancient, twisted railway seat in the stationyard, and all were quietly working away at long white envelopes, which they were carefully opening with razor blades.

'These are our reports,' a spokesman with violent red hair and permanently filthy knees told me. 'The Organ Grinder gave them to us tonight after practice.' He used with rough affection the title by which my friend was known to his choir.

He bent close over the razor blade and moved it expertly. 'If you just lift this little bottom flap,' he explained, 'you can open the envelope, and when you've read the report you tuck the flap in and it doesn't look as though the envelope's ever been mucked about with at all.'

'But *you're* not supposed to read the report,' I remonstrated.

'It's always best to,' said Red Head sagely. 'You've got to know what the Organ Grinder's saying about you.'

'But you've still got to hand in the report to your parents,' I pointed out.

'Yes,' he agreed, with perhaps a shade of pity in his tone for my unbelievable obtuseness, 'but if it's a rotten one I can take in some flowers for my mum.'

'Well, you'd better hop over into the vicar's garden and get a great big bunch,' put in another boy who had just cut his finger on his razor blade and was smearing blood all over his white shirt, 'because your mum said that if she got any more "room for improvements" you were going to cop it hot and strong.'

'Vicar's garden?' I echoed. 'You're going to get flowers from the vicar's garden?'

'Yes,' explained Red Head. 'There's a big shed half way down the path, and if you go for the flowers behind that the vicar can't see you very well from his study. It's dead safe. You can't afford to take any chances with the vicar. He's got a way of coming round to see your mum and telling all kinds of tales. He only comes round when he wants to complain about you.'

'He doesn't!' squeaked a rotund lad wearing large glasses and a microscopic school cap. 'He came round to our house when my grandfather was ill with smoker's cough.'

'He didn't *know* your grandfather was ill with smoker's cough,' countered Red Head. 'He was after some money for the new organ-blower, and it just *happened* that your grandfather was ill with smoker's cough. The vicar tried to make *everybody* pay up for the organ-blower. He even asked that old Major Something-or-other who sits in the front pew and glares at us, and he hardly *ever* talks to *him* because he keeps on saying we ought to sing "Onward, Christian soldiers" and the vicar can't stand it. And another thing . . .'

'Why don't you shut *up* for a minute?' bawled a rather diminutive urchin on the end of the seat. 'In my report it says that my behaviour couldn't be improved upon.'

'That's true,' agreed the boy who had cut his finger, who had been surveying his blood-spattered shirt with the utmost pride. 'Yes, I reckon that's true all right – the way you go creeping round the Organ Grinder offering to do all the rotten solos, and staying behind after service to practise 'em – just because you can read music.'

Indignation at the downright disgrace of having a colleague in the choir who could read music and wanted to sing solos was abruptly banished by a sharp, conspiratorial hiss from Red Head. 'Look out! There's Julius Caesar! The vicar must be coming!'

Julius Caesar padded into our midst, endeavouring to wag his minute tail with such gleeful vigour that he wagged his whole body. The boys crowded round him in boisterous greeting, with not a long white envelope in sight. The vicar's prize boxer was a great friend of theirs. He managed to get into even more trouble than they did, and was indeed their hero.

The vicar strode purposefully into view, a giant of a man swinging a knobbly stick, and wearing ancient baggy flannel trousers and a hairy sports coat with bulbous leather buttons. He smiled grimly at the boys, ordered them not to hang about the stationyard making nuisances of themselves, and invited me with great determination to go along to the vicarage with him for a cup of coffee before continuing to the house of the friend with whom I was staying.

I was rather sorry about this because the vicar always served up coffee of the most atrocious kind to everyone including those who, like myself, preferred tea. And to make matters worse he always insisted on everyone having a second cup.

The choirboys scuttled away in one direction and we bustled off in the other with Julius Caesar, casting many a longing look behind, at our heels.

The vicar was booming away about the choirboys. 'You've got to show 'em who's *master*,' he was declaring, his stick swinging dangerously. He ran on and on. The idea that he was masterful seemed to fascinate him. He enlarged on his subject and became eloquent. He took even longer and more purposeful strides. Finally, as we reached the Vicarage, he announced, 'We've got the upper hand now, anyway. We send home reports every quarter. Keeps them on their toes all right, I can tell you!'

He opened the imposing Victorian gothic front door by pulling at a piece of string which dangled through the letter box. He directed me to his study and clumped down some stone stairs into a vast, cellar-like region in search of the coffee.

I sat looking out of the open french windows of the study on to a splendid garden – a long garden filled, it seemed, with flowers of every description and colour and perfume. The summer evening was warm and still. The whole world seemed so peaceful and pleasant.

Suddenly Julius Caesar, who had lumbered into the room after me, began to agitate his tiny tail again with tremendous enthusiasm, and his whole body quivered with some secret excitement. His delightfully squashed face wrinkled into what I can only describe as a smile of pure joy.

He was watching a spot at the bottom of the garden beyond a large shed. The flowers there were in even greater profusion than those nearer the house. And a whole mass of them appeared to be

walking towards the fence. As I watched, they hoisted themselves over the fence and were gone.

The vicar arrived with the coffee – a great thick jug of it. He regarded Julius Caesar with puzzlement. 'I sometimes wonder if he's *all right*,' he said. 'Look at that fatuous expression on his face. He doesn't seem to be *with* us. It often happens when he's in this room. I think he must be *stupid*.'

He started to pour the atrocious liquid. 'Ah, as I was saying,' he boomed confidently, 'we've got the choirboys *right* where we want them . . .'

19

Democracy and All That

The new vicar at the country church where my cousin Harry has been in the choir for fifty years is very good at getting his own way. He's very democratic about it. He calls frequent and regular consultation meetings at which all members of the congregation are urged to attend because, as he points out, the running of the parish must be in the hands of the parishioners and not dictated by the views of the clergy. At the meetings everybody sits in a circle so that no one appears more prominent than anyone else and the vicar then opens the consultation by firmly stating his views in detail and at a great length. There then follows a short period in which he welcomes and applauds the views of anyone he can persuade to agree with him ('Yes, indeed! Exactly! Splendid!') and advises the large number who don't agree with him, or don't know what he's talking about, that it is their Christian duty to forego their own views for the sake of progress, unity and the common good of the church. He then neatly rounds off the proceedings with a quick grace and a cup of coffee and everybody gets off for home nice and early.

Thus it was, very belatedly, that the parishioners ('You are in charge. I'm here, your vicar, to carry out your wishes') realized that they had somehow sanctioned the abandoning of a much-loved hymnbook, the huge expense of replacing the church's 'quite dreadful Victorian East window' with modern tinted glass ('So beautiful, restful and simple'), replaced Sunday evensong with a 'Happy Christian Hour' and introduced a children's gnome village and goldfish pond among the listed eighteenth-century tombs in the churchyard.

And it was only when the vicar, racing ahead with reforms, announced the plan ('after a full and detailed discussion') to do away with the outmoded Victorian institution of robed choirs 'cluttering up our fine mediaeval chancel' that the congregation began to be vaguely aware that there was something amiss somewhere in the democratic system. The choir themselves were mostly seasoned veterans who, over recent years, had become thoroughly used to a succession of vicars, each of whom arrived in the parish full of enthusiasm and radical thoughts, intent on sweeping away the moribund ideas of his predecessor and dragging the church from the nineteenth century to transform it into an up-to-the-minute, relevant, meaningful body – a vital community. The snag was that the various vicars' notions of how to achieve all this differed so widely and each had stayed in the parish for such a short time before deciding that the whole place was beyond any kind of help, democratic or otherwise, that the parishioners, when they tried to envisage anything beyond what they'd always done, carried on supremely, happily unconcerned – until the vicar's latest bombshell.

On the Sunday evening after the parishioners learned that they had made the decision to remove the choir from the chancel, the choir held an emergency meeting in the back room of the Charging Bull with cousin Harry in the chair. Normally at choir meetings the organist took the chair, but on this occasion the thought of the democratic decision he had apparently helped to make had so upset him that it was felt that he was not really the best person to conduct this meeting in view of the somewhat rude, indeed violent, language he was tending to use in front of the choirgirls whenever the vicar was mentioned. So, spluttering pipe clamped in a corner of his mouth, he sat at the back of the room under a violently rolling cloud of smoke, muttering awful threats.

Cousin Harry sat at a rickety card-table behind a tankard of beer and attempted to field questions and suggestions here and there that he could disentangle from the boxing-ring racket of everyone shouting at once. 'He says we've decided that the choir won't wear robes any more and they'll sit in with the congregation,' he bawled. 'He says we're one united family which we can't be with the choir stuck up the steps behind the screen.' Cousin Harry was careful not actually to mention the vicar's name in view of the trouble they were having with the organist.

'Well, all that's out for a start,' thundered the principal bass, a huge gentleman blocking everyone's view in the middle of the front row. He could be heard easily even at this meeting because, without really trying, he could drown out all other sounds for hundreds of yards around. That's why he was principal bass. The hubbub ceased and everyone turned in his direction. 'We've always been robed. We've always been in the chancel.' His clenched fist shot up dramatically in the direction of a broken light fitting that hung drunkenly from the ceiling. 'That's where we belong. That's where we stay!'

'He says robed chairs in the chancel are an out-moded Victorian idea,' put in an indignant little man from under the bass's arm. 'He says, before that, choirs wore ordinary clothes and were hidden away in the gallery with a double bass fiddle and a flute or something!'

'It'll be even worse than that now,' took up a prominent-looking contralto lady with blue hair and lots of bangles. She raised a hand, pointing imperiously at Cousin Harry as the bangles clattered musically down her arm. 'If he thinks I'm going to sit down in the congregation with all those people who can't sing and their kids running up and down the pews, bawling, he's got another thing coming, united family or no united family.'

A man who had not joined in the general fray but had been sitting quietly solving the *Sunday Times* crossword puzzle now spoke. He looked remarkably like Beniamino Gigli and was indeed the choir's leading tenor. 'There's no immediate worry,' he assured silkily. 'He can't push us out that easily.'

'He'll need a faculty to get rid of *us*,' countered the huge bass. 'He says we're to sit down in the congregation from next Sunday. He says it's going to be a real family get-together. There are some christenings – three babies and a man of eighty-five who missed out earlier – and some jolly praise songs.'

'Heaven help us,' groaned Blue Hair.

'There's not much chance of that,' rumbled the huge bass. 'We'll have to help ourselves.'

Gigli smiled and spoke smoothly. 'It'll all blow over. We've had this kind of thing before. There was that vicar chap before the last one. He tried it the other way round. He wanted the congregation to sit in the choirstalls with the choir. It's this family thing these modern clerics have got sold on. Everybody's got to be massed together and shaking hands.'

The smoke around the organist had by now completely enveloped him and was threatening to obscure the rest of the protesters. There was no doubt the organist was becoming very upset . . .

Thus far into the crisis I learned from letters from Cousin Harry, who likes to keep me in touch with the goings-on at his church, as I like to keep him in touch with goings-on at mine. Then, as usual, came my invitation for my once-yearly visit, when traditionally I was a guest in the choir and sat next to Cousin Harry, who brought me up to date in detail with parish politics in a penetrating, hissing whisper right through both lessons and the sermon at matins.

Apparently the vicar's dreamed-of-service when everyone – congregation, choir and Gigli's cat Rossini – sat together as a family took place on the Sunday morning before my visit and the vicar's ecstasy lasted through the rest of the day and until the Monday evening, when a deputation from the parish called at the vicarage to say that, despite the importance of the family spirit, the general feeling was that the choir should stay firmly in the choirstalls. A dozen members of the congregation were afraid the choir would displace them from their favourite seats behind pillars or next to radiators, others agreed that although the principal bass's voice sounded fine and stirring from the choirstalls, it tended only to stir up trouble in the pews where it frightened the young children. Yet others objected to choir members passing round foul-smelling throat lozenges throughout the service or reading paperbacks during the sermon. So by and large the congregation felt strongly that the choir should be in the choirstalls where they'd always been and could do no harm. It seemed right and proper.

Finally a very enterprising member of the congregation, who was considered an expert on the history of the village church because, from time to time, he produced articles about it in the parish magazine which he'd copied word for word from books in the public library, discovered during his researches that the choir were not in fact 'cluttering up the fine mediaeval chancel', as the vicar had alleged. The fine mediaeval chancel had apparently fallen down in the middle of the eighteenth century and the present one was a replacement built in 1887 to commemorate Queen Victoria's golden jubilee.

The vicar recognizes when he has been outmanoeuvred. He doesn't cry over spilled milk. He forges ahead regardless. Cousin Harry tells me that his latest call for a full parish meeting is to enable everyone to decide democratically that the pews be removed and be replaced with tip-up, cinema-style seats. Alas for democracy. The parishioners have learned their lesson. Plans for a protest march to the vicarage are already under way.

20

Mud

In my uncle's parish the Men's Fellowship really get down to *doing* things. They've got a dynamic vicar who makes sure that they do.

During the period of my latest visit to the village, the Fellowship's main preoccupation was the moving of about twenty tons of earth from in front of the windows of two disused and derelict basement rooms at the vicarage. This was to enable the vicar to lure a new bachelor curate to the parish by holding out the bait of a light, attractive lower ground floor flat. There *was* other accommodation nearby which would have suited a go-ahead young curate. There was, for instance, a delightful bijou Regency-type ruin with no electric light or main drainage, which was going for a mere fortune; or a very handy flat in a modern rabbit-hutch villa with warped windowframes and leaking roof, for only ninety pounds a week. This *did* have electric light, which was readily available by placing dozens of coins into a slot meter every night. Or one could always suffer discreetly in the genteel boarding establishment of the lady in perpetual black who came regularly to church once a year on the anniversary of her marriage to her late husband. She never failed to put her fifty penny bit in the plate and never failed to complain that the church was cold.

However, the vicar decided that it would be better for the young curate to be under his wing at the vicarage, and such were his powers of description that the curate had actually *seen* an ideal bachelor flat where our uninspired eyes saw only the two coal-cellar-like pits. So now, as the summer rain steadily fell, we worked to make the dream come true.

I don't know quite how it happened, but someone had passed to me one of those gigantic steel barrows that have a single iron wheel and weigh so much that you can't move them even when they are empty. My job was to load up the earth that the others dug away from the basement windows, and dump it at the bottom of the vicarage garden where the youth club was going to start a rockery. For some unfathomable reason, the only way to reach the spot was to cross a goldfish pond by means of a four-inch wide sagging board which was covered by mud. Mud was everywhere in generous quantities, particularly in my monstrous barrow as I tried to plough across the chaos of the garden.

Now, I have never been much good at managing one-wheeled barrows full of mud, especially when they have to be pushed along slimy planks and over-yawning goldfish ponds. The only way to manoeuvre such a burden, I felt, was to get up a good speed, aim the barrow at the plank and hope for the best.

I did it! I crossed the pond in splendid style, but the effort made it impossible for me to prevent the barrow tipping prematurely and hurling its contents all over the vicar's pansies. The vicar saw the whole thing. In fact he was only a few feet away, urging me on. He never showed the slightest annoyance. I certainly saw his Christian spirit hard at work then. He just shouted that it was a jolly good try and would I like to go across to the other side of the garden and do a bit of weeding. A little mishap like buried prize pansies didn't deter him for a moment. A single glance at him revealed that he was a dynamic vicar. He was a big man with a jutting jaw and outsized horn-rimmed glasses. He never rested himself and made sure that nobody else did either. He kept on issuing vital calls and stirring challenges, and unlike many dynamic vicars who have this habit, he actually took part in much of the manual work they entailed. He was there, with his men, working more rigorously than any of them. He never seemed to tire. My uncle said that he didn't know his own strength and that any job with which he helped took twice as long because of all the making good that had to be done in the wake of his tremendous efforts.

After I had been quietly weeding for some time in a bed of rosebushes and stinging nettles, the vicar's wife wheeled out her latest addition to the family, a chubby bald-headed infant in a pram full of sticky, coloured plastic bricks, empty cigarette cartons and a one-eyed, threadbare teddy bear. She said perhaps I'd be kind enough to keep an eye on the bald-headed infant, and retreated hastily, all smiles and thanks. This definitely slowed down the weeding process because my charge had the curious habit of hurling the teddy bear at me and screaming his head off until I retrieved it for him. And immediately I obliged we started the whole routine all over again. The situation soon became rather frustrating but was still, I congratulated myself, infinitely better than the barrows of mud or, indeed, the rosebushes and stinging nettles, and before long

I found myself devoting all my attention to the teddy bear tussle. The infant was as tireless as his father. By the time his mother came again to collect him he had thrown not only the bear, but everything else movable in his pram, including the shade and part of the pushing handle. I refixed these to the best of my ability and the vicar's wife was again all smiles and thanks. She said the vicar had to refix them about twenty times a day, but he took much longer than I had because he was not mechanically minded and just didn't understand.

We looked across to where the vicar had just upset a barrow of mud on precisely the same prize pansies that had suffered through my mishap. And then for the first time I noticed that no one appeared to be digging round the basement windows. Except for the vicar the site was empty.

'It's a lorry out in front of the vicarage,' explained the vicar's wife. 'It's developed a flat tyre and one or two planks have fallen off into the road. The men are all out there helping.' She surveyed the abandoned spades and pick-axes in the streaming mud. 'Well, that's what the Men's Fellowship is *for* after all,' she declared, 'to help.'

The vicar plunged through the flowerbed to me. 'State of emergency!' he bellowed. 'If I carry on

with the actual *carting*, perhaps you'll just potter around for a bit with the digging,' he asked, and he handed me the biggest pick-axe I had ever seen. The job on the lorry seemed to take a very long while indeed. I pottered around with the digging till it became too dark to see whether I was still removing the earth or part of the brickwork of the vicarage. Then, while the vicar, dynamic as ever, was on his way across the goldfish pond with the last load, I raised myself slowly on my pick-axe and stumbled quietly away.

In the road outside there was no sign of the lorry, but the members of the Men's Fellowship were still there in earnest discussion. One of them kindly enquired if I felt all right. He said they'd all been very busy helping the lorry driver . . .

The young bachelor curate never took the lower ground floor flat after all. He got married unexpectedly and it would not have been large enough. He was eventually given a living in a parish with a nice big Victorian vicarage with enough room to house a regiment, and standing in acres of grounds where no human foot had trod for years. He too formed a Men's Fellowship.

21

Sack the Lot!

The church choir in which I sang as a guest a few months ago was a downright disgrace. The vicar didn't think so, and the organist didn't think so, but the Parochial Church Council did. And I had arrived at their ancient village church, somewhere in Norfolk, at a most crucial moment. As I robed for Sunday matins my uncle, who had introduced me to the church, told me about the awful row at the last PCC meeting. It was all started by a very respected member of the congregation, who had slept in the front pew for years. It appeared that lately, whenever he opened his eyes they fell upon the sight of choirboys twisting each others' arms, and the choirmen making eyes at the choirgirls. He had stood this for a considerable time without complaint, he said, but now felt compelled to bring the matter to the notice of the PCC.

The PCC, who for the last six meetings had been bored stiff by completely non-productive discussions on the renewing of the church's lethal electricity system and the replacing of the vicar's veteran kitchen range, were only too pleased to welcome a little variety by having a go at the choir. It was always pleasant to have a go at the choir, anyway.

One man, who had been firmly rejected as a chorister owing to the fog-horn quality of his voice, rose to support the front-pew sleeper. Far be it from him, he said, to criticize the choir, but discipline must be maintained. When he was principal bass of the Little Withering Choral Society the discipline was *most* strict. He then recited a whole list of choral societies where the discipline had been most strict, and where, incidentally, he had also been principal bass. Judging by the large number, one gained the impression that he had been handed over from one society to another with the utmost haste until he'd encountered a brick wall in the shape of our unappreciative village choirmaster.

This speaker was now rapidly backed up by the local retired colonel. The colonel, who always made a speech at church council meetings whether he had anything to say or not, and always started off with 'Of course, in *my* day . . .', ranted on for a quarter of an hour, finally working himself up to a stirring call to 'sack the lot!'

No one took much notice of him, because he was always sacking some lot or other, but when the village postmistress took the floor there was a sudden respectful attention. It didn't pay to ignore this frail little lady, who by her very calling knew more about everyone's business than they knew themselves. Experience showed that it was far better to humour a character who knew all about you, and who kept the only shop for miles.

She said demurely that the whole thing made her blush with shame. To think that members of the choir above *all* could act in such an abandoned manner ... She felt that a sub-committee must be formed immediately to deal with the emergency. She revelled in sub-committees. Members met almost daily over her counter, between intervals of obtaining stamps, bacon and family allowances.

The postmistress was followed eagerly by more members, who stumbled incoherently over words which they fondly imagined to be devastating broadsides at the choir. But the vicar, ever faithful to his singers, had managed to delay any definite decision – he was very good at delaying definite decisions – until members of the council had had one more opportunity to observe the choir on Sunday morning. So now the test was at hand, and the choir filed slowly into church, the organist's plea not to twist each others' arms or make eyes at each other fresh in our ears.

The church was packed. Every single member of the PCC had made a special effort to be there. Indeed, I learned later that one member was so concerned over the shameful slackness of the choir that he had even foregone his customary Sunday trip to the coast in order to keep an eye on them. The vicar regarded the choir nervously, obviously hoping that on this occasion they would heed his oft-repeated – and ignored – warning about keeping their voices down during the service, particularly in the parts where only he was supposed to be speaking.

He need not have worried. The choir was sphinx-like. The anthem was Elvey's 'I was glad when they said unto me, we will go into the House of Lord', and when they came to the passage, 'peace be within thy walls' – the composer repeats the word 'peace' softly, several times in succession – it seemed that the whole congregation were lulled into a false sense of well-being. The PCC members looked particularly shamefaced as they shuffled down the aisle at the conclusion of the service. In fact, one of the more gullible members, a lady who was now feeling very guilty over the churlish manner in which she had attacked the choir at the meeting, went round to the vestry in order to congratulate the boys on their exemplary behaviour. Most of them had already disappeared, lightheartedly gambolling across the vicar's kitchen garden, but the organist managed to locate two who were locked in a death struggle in the churchyard. Hastily separating them and wiping away the blood, he presented them to the lady, who beamed on them, shook their filthy hands, and went away with a conscience much eased.

Only the colonel, who hadn't liked the hymns and didn't agree with the sermon, stuck to his guns. As my uncle and I passed within earshot he was declaiming to a rapidly diminishing audience, 'Sack the lot! Why, in my day . . .'

22

Not to be Taken Away

The gallery of this village church had always been a nuisance. In the mid-nineteenth century it had been pulled down in memory of someone's grandfather who had got mixed up in the Indian Mutiny, and in the late nineteenth century it had been put back again in memory of someone else's maiden aunt who had spent most of her life trying to close all the local pubs.

In those days the choir and the organ were housed in the gallery, but nowadays the choir was accommodated in the chancel and the organist was left up there on his own. He was always complaining. He said he couldn't see the choir and could hardly even hear them and, even when he did, they were always a beat or two behind the organ.

Besides, he was most upset about the mice. He reckoned that during the services they kept on scurrying past and glaring at him, and some had grown so defiant that they even ambled across the top of the console during the most difficult part of the anthem. He said the whole thing was most disconcerting.

And now it had been discovered that a generous amount of dry rot had crept into the supporting timbers of the gallery, and the church architect had announced firmly that the Parochial Church Council would either have to spend a great deal on repairs or pull the whole thing down again. He enjoyed announcing things firmly to the Parochial Church Council, and particularly to the vicar. The architect was the expert on the subject, and it compensated him for the many times the vicar implied that *he* was the expert on music, and kept on changing all the architect's favourite Victorian hymn tunes.

Of course, the church council, in the manner of church councils when faced with an urgent problem requiring a concerted effort, immediately split into two violently opposing camps. Those who wanted to do away with the gallery accused the opposition of being non-progressive stick-in-the-muds, and those who wanted to keep it talked of vicious vandalism. Then there was a small group who tried to pour oil on troubled waters by announcing with beautiful helpful smiles to members of both the main parties that the gallery didn't really matter at all because the church was not a building: it was people – people all pulling together in one great united body.

But they didn't make much of an impression. The church architect said that if the gallery fell down on the great united body as it was coming into church for evensong one Sunday night, it would probably matter a great deal . . .

Finding myself in the vicinity of the village one gentle summer afternoon, and having heard of the great gallery controversy from a correspondent who loves to report to me such parish-shaking events, I decided to see the gallery for myself before the Parochial Church Council or dry rot banished it for ever.

But the first thing that I saw as I entered the church was not the gallery but a patch of unbridled chaos in the centre aisle. It consisted of a beanpole-like lady of uncertain age enveloped in an electric-blue smock and standing before an easel and large canvas. All around her were paint tins and multi-coloured rags, and beneath her large, brogue-shod feet were spread about a dozen back numbers of *The Times*, all freely oozing paint. On a nearby pew stood a battered vacuum flask and a mug with no handle and, on another pew, a pile of cheese sand-wiches and squashed jam tarts.

I made as little disturbance as possible, and moved along a side aisle to get a better view of the gallery. Apart from a furious glance the beanpole lady took no notice of me. Every so often she would glare up at the gallery, make sharp little tutting noises, and ram her brush into the canvas.

Curiosity got the better of me. I tiptoed across the church and stood behind her to view her picture. It was one of those very advanced and deep efforts, where you are supposed to know what was in the mind of the artist at the time of painting.

The background was a bilious shade of mauve, except towards the bottom of the canvas where it turned green. In the top left-hand corner there was something that looked like an unfinished game of noughts and crosses, and this in turn gave place to a sort of big sausage which had an eye and three little feet. In the top right-hand corner a three-cornered sun beamed down on a bloated question mark surrounding a hatchet.

The beanpole lady pushed back a wisp of blue hair and transferred her glare from the gallery to me. 'Believe it or not,' she fumed, 'they want to pull down our gallery. This picture will *show* them what the church will look like if they do. I'm going to make them *see*.' She flung a brushful of crimson paint at the one-eyed sausage. 'It's terrible,' she glowered, 'terrible!'

I never like to be rude about other people's particular talents, so I said I didn't think it was as bad as all that. But of course she was referring to the idea of pulling down the gallery, not to her effort at representing the consequences pictorially, so she immediately classed me as one of the anti-gallery group and refused to speak to me again.

Seating myself in a front pew I turned and contemplated the gallery. Perhaps the beanpole lady's picture would save it. The picture was even more horrible to look at than the gallery, and if people really took the picture seriously ... I remembered then from my correspondent that there was in fact one other picture of the church without the gallery, but that would never be openly shown. It was a picture taken in the very early days of photography, and showed the figure of a gentleman with an enormous black beard and drainpipe trousers, who was apparently pointing to where the gallery was going to be built.

The trouble was that in those days you had to stand perfectly still and hold your breath until you were blue in the face when being photographed. And this gentleman had obviously moved his arm two or three times during the process, so that in the picture he looked like a kind of human octopus with arms all round his body. Also, because of the particular angle from which the photograph had been taken, it appeared that he was supporting on his head a five-hundredweight angel which drooped over someone's memorial on the wall at the back of the church.

Unfortunately the gentleman had been the great-uncle of a very respectable and terrifyingly humourless Rear Admiral (RN Retired) who was a prominent member of the present-day congregation, and consequently the photograph was kept strictly out of public view.

Sometimes during a particularly long sermon by a very keen visiting preacher, or when the Rear Admiral had complained yet again about the disgraceful behaviour of the choir, the organist would take it out of its hiding place in the music cupboard and enjoy a little snigger, but most people agreed that he had a rather twisted sense of humour.

The gallery frowned on me. It was a hefty erection of dark brown varnished panels and cracked plaster, and supported on its front a timeless kitchen clock with one hand and no glass. The bean-pole lady made a louder-than-usual tutting noise, and rammed her brush at the canvas with even greater ferocity.

With a joyous clatter of pedals, the organ roared forth into one of the jolliest tunes I had ever heard inside or outside a church. It was thrilling. It was splendid. I bounded up the gallery stairs and looked round a green baize curtain for the purveyor of this uplifting sound. The organist swept his hands from the keyboard and turned. I'd never seen such a gloomy man.

'I'd like to see the whole lot pulled down,' he grated, after I had congratulated him on his playing. 'I don't know why I stay here. Can't see the choir, mice and dry rot all over the place – pull the lot down is what I day.' He contemplated a mousehole almost under the pedals. 'I've tried to bung that up, but they still come through.' His expressed an even deeper gloom. He started to play again, and the tune sounded jollier than ever.

In the churchyard I met the vicar, a tall, thin, middle-aged bachelor, with a gentle, far-away look and dirty shoes with the laces untied. He was most interested to learn that I was a chorister.

'Of course, we have a good choir here,' he

remarked vaguely, half to me and half to a large red tabby cat who sat sunning himself on a tombstone, 'but they sing the wrong *kind* of music – so *loud*, so *obvious*. There is so much *good* music available nowadays – *worthwhile*, simple, beautiful music – but I can't seem to make them *realize*. An uphill task, I'm afraid, an uphill task . . .'

I broached the parish-shaking question of the gallery. The vicar was gazing admiringly at the cat. 'You know, he's a very fine specimen,' he mused. 'No white on him at all. A perfect British red tabby – the gallery, you were saying? Yes, there is some little difficulty there, I believe.' He beamed quite serenely. 'There is always something. But it passes, it passes.'

Gusts of the organist's jolly tune reached us as we neared the church door. Some of the serenity left the vicar's beam. 'Oh, dear,' he murmured regretfully, 'oh, dear. A good fellow, but – oh, dear.'

23

Too Much of a Good Thing

My Aunt Ada has no particular political leanings. She says there's not much to choose between the parties, anyway. They're all run by politicians so what can you expect? She has, however, a number of friends who are very politically minded and between them actively support most of the established parties. But despite their political differences, which they thoroughly relish, there is one thing on which they all agree. Aunt Ada's home-made marmalade is the finest to be had anywhere. Accordingly, whenever they are planning their respective fund-raising functions they never fail to ask Aunt Ada for as many jars of her marmalade as she will give them and in return, knowing her one great weakness, they ply her with numerous boxes of exotic chocolates. So, throughout the year, Aunt Ada's kitchen shelves are alternately crammed with pounds and pounds of marmalade and pounds and pounds of chocolates. And always, towards the end of the year, there comes a time when even Aunt Ada can't cope with the huge surplus of chocolates. Then it is that the village church choir profits. Aunt Ada sends the organist a great suitcase of boxes of the most mouth-watering creations which he then lays about the vestry on every suitable surface just before Sunday matins. Some years ago it was his practice to place on each box a little card inviting 'Take some' but these days everyone knows the drill and he leaves the chocolates to invite for themselves.

It was at the time of the latest of these occasions that I was spending a weekend break with Aunt Ada and arrived bright and early at the church to sing in the choir of which I am a sort of honorary member.

Four or five choirboys were scrabbling vigorously about the vestry floor that covered the holey carpet around a pedestal supporting a black marble bust of a demonic-looking eighteenth-century vicar of the parish. Someone had moved it out of the back of the church as not being really suitable for the children's corner that had recently built up around it. I had obviously just missed the stage where there had been some misunderstanding as to who should open the chocolates, and the box had been unequal to the strain. It now lay, a crumpled wreck, all rosettes and ribbon, in the middle of the floor.

As I sought to avoid a churned-up mass of strawberry cremes and lime surprises that plainly the boys had not avoided, I backed into the solid form of the organist, who was just arriving; a rotund, comfortably middle-aged man with a cheeky schoolboy face and tiny chubby hands that you would have thought could hardly manage a keyboard. He cast a smiling glance at the scrabbling chocolate-gatherers and made purposefully for another box of chocolates that he'd earlier placed on top of the piano. This time the label caught his eye. 'Ah!' he sighed, disappointed. 'Hard centres. I don't like those. Here, have some.' As he handed me the box a huge hand appeared over my shoulder and scooped up a fistful of the sweetmeats and the large voice of our large bass soloist rumbled in my ear. 'Well, what do you think about this government *now*?' He always asked the same question as he walked into the vestry on Sunday morning. No one ever tried to answer him because he obviously never expected an answer, always carrying on immediately about the trouble he was having with his garden or his car or his mother-in-law and not expecting a rejoinder about these either. He talked continuously. No one took any notice of what he said but the sound of his rich dark-brown voice created a friendly, comfortable atmosphere that we all enjoyed.

On this particular Sunday this atmosphere was enhanced by Aunt Ada's chocolates, and the choirboys and three or four of the men having filled their cassock pockets with them, we processed into church under the baleful eye of the vicar who didn't like chocolates because they inevitably upset his stomach and didn't like the choir for the same reason.

All went happily as usual until, during the reading of the second lesson, a small chorister called Percy, sitting at the end of the choirstall in front of me, craned round and, presenting a bright green face to me, announced in a dramatic whisper 'I'm going to be sick. They weren't very nice chocolates. I'm going to be ever so sick.' The boy next to him, in loud tones of disgust, advised me, 'Take no notice of him. He always does this when the weather's fine. He wants to be excused so he can go fishing.'

'His face is green,' I said. 'He's not going fishing – he's going to be sick.'

I went outside with Percy and he quickly disappeared into the back regions of the churchyard

185

among the sadly neglected eighteenth-century tombs and the even more sadly neglected modern dustbins. Within minutes he was back looking much better without his green facial hue. Extracting a large biliously pink piece of nougat from his cassock pocket (which by the look of it had been there long before the chocolates) and biting off at least half of it, he assured me he was now recovered enough to go back into the choir for the rest of the service. As he spoke, another chorister with a green face stumbled into the vestry from the chancel. Percy looked concerned and offered him the remains of his nougat and seemed surprised when his friend accelerated past him into the churchyard without so much as a word of thanks.

Prayers were now being said in church so I suggested that we wait until the next hymn before going back to our places. Percy agreed and started wandering around the vestry selecting chocolates here and there and slipping them into his cassock pocket. 'I think it was the coffee creme ones that were bad,' he pronounced. 'I've not taken any of those this time. These'll be all right for evensong.'

He chewed contentedly and studied a row of framed paintings and photographs of former vicars of the parish. 'These are all old vicars,' he explained. 'Old vicars weren't very jolly – they never smiled.' He pointed to the evidence. 'Look at 'em. You can see they never smiled.'

'Perhaps they had to put up with a terrible lot of choirboys like you lot,' I suggested.

He considered this possibility. 'I don't think so,' he decided. 'The boys must have been pretty good in those days. All the men in our family for years and years have been in the choir and my grandfather says that in his day you got a good hiding if you came to church with even a little speck of mud on your shoes and it was even worse if you had dirty nails or hadn't washed your neck.'

'Who gave the good hidings?' I asked, intrigued. 'The choirmaster or the vicar – or your father?'

He bit into an outsized chocolate creme. 'Oh, the choirmaster,' he confirmed. 'And my grandfather says you got a good hiding from your father as well if he found out that you'd had a good hiding from the choirmaster. The vicar didn't give good hidings. He just said it served you right when you got one and perhaps you'd now behave a little less like a savage.'

'So choirboys were better behaved years ago?' I asked. Percy carefully selected another chocolate from a handful that still included the partially consumed pink nougat. He chewed, and seemed satisfied. 'Well, it's harder these days – being what they call good, I mean.'

'Modern life!' I said.

'It's girls,' he amended. 'Girls are the trouble.'

'Ah!' I said.

'Girls!' He warmed to his subject. 'You see, the vicar suddenly wanted to have girls in the choir – you know how vicars suddenly want to have things and then get all cross and upset when some people don't want 'em. Well, anyway, the choirmen had a meeting in the Red Lion one Sunday after matins and my Uncle Fred says they were all furious.'

'Of course,' I sympathized. 'They didn't like the idea of girls in the choir.'

'My Uncle Fred said over their dead bodies,' confirmed Percy, 'so that was that.'

'Exactly,' I said.

Percy looked indignant. 'So now the vicar puts all the girls in the front row of the congregation and says they're his reserve choir and they try to drown us.'

'And what do you all think of that?' I asked.

He ignored the question. 'These girls keep on

making faces at us so we make faces back and the vicar says we're the worst lot of choirboys that he's ever had. So it's these girls that are the trouble, you see. The boys had nothing like that to put up with in the days of the old vicars.'

The second victim of the chocolates now returned to the vestry, looking the picture of health and eating from a handful of blackberries. 'There's tons of them along the back wall,' he enthused. 'Here, try some.'

Percy tried some. 'You've got a great big blackberry stain on your surplice,' he said, and, turning to me, 'He'd have got a good hiding for that all right in the days of the old vicars.'

The first verse of the next hymn now sounded and the three of us discreetly returned to the choirstalls. Not so discreetly, however, as not to be noticed by Aunt Ada. 'What *was* going on in the choirstalls?' she asked me as we walked home.

'Two of the boys felt sick,' I explained. 'It was the chocolates, I'm afraid.'

Aunt Ada sounded as though she couldn't believe her ears. 'But they were *very* superior chocolates,' she said, 'handmade, really very good.'

'I think it was a case of having too much of a good thing,' I said.

After lunch I washed up while Aunt Ada packed three dozen jars of her marmalade ready for collection by the chairman of the 'Save our branch line' campaign. He arrived full of enthusiasm and festooned with badges depicting steam locomotives and traction engines and trams and, having stowed the marmalade in his car boot, presented Aunt Ada with the largest box of chocolates of all I'd seen that day.

Aunt Ada said how lovely but that he really shouldn't and as soon as he had departed suggested firmly that I took them along for the choir when I went to evensong. 'I don't know, though,' she amended. 'We don't want all that messing about in the choirstalls again. I know,' her kindly face lit with pleasure, 'I'll give them to those girls who sit in the front pew – his reserve choir, the vicar calls them. They really do help out with the singing down in the congregation.'

So, just before evensong, Aunt Ada passed the outsized box of chocolates to the girls with whispered instructions not to eat a single one until after the service.

Alas, sweet temptation! Someone opened the box 'just to have a look' and by the time we reached the sermon it had somehow passed up and down the row a dozen times and was all but empty. Quite unaware of the gluttony the vicar climbed into the pulpit, prepared to beam happily down on to his own special choir which he fervently hoped would one day take the place of the hooligans in the choir-stalls. The happy beam never materialized. He gaped in bewilderment at the sea of chocolate wrappings below him and, as he gaped, a large discarded chocolate box slithered into the aisle. One of the girls rose abruptly and scuttled out in a great hurry...

After the service a group of choirboys were looking into the church from the vestry to where the vicar was confronting his reserve choir. 'He looks real mad with them,' observed Percy. 'Just like one of those old vicars.'

'He's mad all right,' agreed a friend, 'even madder than when you left your skateboard at the bottom of the tower steps and he came down in a hurry from winding the clock...'

They watched a little longer. 'Come on,' said Percy, 'he's not going to let up for ages. Something tells me we're not going to be bothered any more with that lot sitting in the front row and making faces at us.'

'I think you're right,' agreed his friend. He

groped in his pocket and produced a handful of decidedly battered chocolates. 'Here, have some,' he invited.

24

Progress Report

A mile or so behind a West Country village which I have known and loved for years, the County Council have built a new six-lane by-pass to relieve the traffic congestion on the village street.

Somehow the county councillors couldn't get out of their heads the idea that the village street wanted relieving. And it was no good the villagers telling the councillors that the congestion which apparently made necessary the thousands of poundsworth of relieving consisted almost entirely of a farmer's horse and cart, the school bus and the vicar's bike. After all, the village street didn't really lead anywhere except to the local historic castle which comprised a piece of shattered wall and a pile of rubble surrounded by little lines of stones set in the grass and marked with Department of the Environment notices saying 'Great Hall' and 'Outer Bailey' and 'No dogs allowed'. But the county councillors had decided that the relieving was necessary and relieving on a grand scale was carried out.

As I entered the village one sunny autumn morning a few weeks after the opening of the by-pass, the same great friendly black retriever was wandering to and fro across the street greeting his many friends as in the pre-by-pass days, and the same horse and cart was parked outside the same pub. The school bus wasn't in sight, but a farm tractor hauling a trolley-load of mangelwurzels had broken down on the wrong side of the road and an ancient lady wearing a floppy hat was sitting in the gutter on a little stool painting a picture of a sort of mediaeval gaol house, of which the villagers were intensely proud, which was leaning so far forward that it threatened to fall into the road at any minute. Everything was very much as it had always been.

As I was passing the local hardware shop the vicar emerged from the broom-festooned doorway carrying a huge bag of garden manure and a tin of cat food. 'Just the man!' he rumbled from somewhere within his comfortable, tweed-clad frame. 'I really wanted to take two bags of manure – really splendid stuff, this – but I couldn't manage both of them at once. Perhaps you'd help me out?'

He shunted backwards into the doorway, booming over his shoulder at an unseen salesman in the shadowy depths of the beansticks and suspended frying pans and kettles, and in no time at all I was fixed up with my load of manure and trying to keep up with the vicar as he rolled down the street at a spanking pace towards the vicarage.

We clambered up a dozen crumbling stone steps to the front door, and it shows how familiarity with surroundings helps when it comes to dragging huge sacks of manure up crumbling vicarage steps. The vicar manoeuvred his sack up with the utmost ease while mine almost over-balanced me on every single step. When I at last arrived triumphantly in the hall, the vicar led the way along a long, lino-covered passage and through a door which gave access to a dozen more steps which went all the way down again. It was not such heavy work getting the manure *down* the steps, of course, but a little difficulty arose owing to the extreme narrowness of the steps. One had somehow to lift the sack before one on the left foot and move forward on the right one, at the same time avoiding knocking off the wall rows of copper warming pans and photos of vintage cars and clergymen's cricket teams.

At the bottom we came upon the vicar's study through which you could reach the garden, but the vicar said we wouldn't take the manure any further until we'd had a cup of tea, so we piled it into the fireplace next to a large pot of paper chrysanthemums.

When he'd brought the tea the vicar turned to the subject of the new by-pass. He said he had recently made three quite unsuccessful attempts to write something interesting about it for the parish magazine. 'You see,' he explained, 'I like to keep the magazine up to the minute and right abreast of local events, but although the by-pass is in our vicinity it really has nothing whatsoever to do with us.' He pointed out that it skirted both the villages of which he was vicar and there was still only a farm road and an overgrown public footpath which connected the two. 'And even they are not very busy except when there happens to be a fifth Sunday in the month. They are generally quite busy then.' This strange fact, announced in such a matter-of-fact manner interested me considerably. I wanted to know more. And of course, when it was explained to me, everything proved to be so simple and understandable.

The vicar was in charge of a combined parish and, owing to the lack of curates and the curious reluctance of the available ones to take a post in which they would never again be heard of in the outside world, he had been obliged to conduct matins in one village church and evensong in the other on the first and third Sundays and vice versa on the second and fourth Sundays. This plan worked well and the congregation quite happily made the necessary journeys to each others' villages.

But no one quite knew where to go when there was a fifth Sunday in the month. Consequently on a fifth Sunday not one village but both were on the move, and members of the combined congregations would meet each other on the farm road and overgrown footpath, going in opposite directions for the same service. And when they met they were never able to agree on who was going to the right church, and would carry on in their chosen directions. Then those who were right were able to attend the service, and those who were wrong and found the church shut simply turned into the local tavern, or pressed their company on to any nearby friends or relations who happened to be at home.

'Nevertheless,' continued the vicar with a sudden enthusiasm, as if he had just thought a thrilling thought, 'I really do think that eventually the bypass will do us a world of good. I mean, it's bringing *civilization* to the place. It will attract *attention* to us.'

I had a startling vision of thousands of suicidal drivers in high-powered cars tearing into the village and pulling up all over the place to gaze in amazement at the locals. 'You may be right,' I agreed.

'Oh, I'm quite sure I am,' boomed the vicar. 'I'm sure I am.' The idea gripped him. He produced his pipe and knocked it out so hard that his china ashtray broke in half. 'Do you know,' he confided, sweeping the wreck of the ashtray into the pot of paper chrysanthemums, 'I've advertised solidly for *months* in *all* the church newspapers for a curate. *Today* I got a reply! Yes, the by-pass is going to open us up. People are coming in!'

I think that by now he'd forgotten I was there because, although he'd poured out his own tea, he hadn't poured out mine and there didn't seem to be a cup for me anyway. There were some biscuits but he didn't offer me one, and I couldn't take one because he was grasping the tin tightly to him and talking most encouragingly of the great village renaissance.

Some time later the vicar remembered the presence of the manure, and me, and suggested that perhaps it would be a good idea to get the manure down into the shed. Then, noting that it was almost dark, he hurriedly helped himself to another biscuit and announced that he really must nip across to the church to tell the choirmaster the good news of the curate. 'Choir practice will just about be over,' he explained, urging me along the lino-covered passage and up the steps again. 'I'm sure you'd like to see our choirmaster again.'

We entered the vestry as the choirmaster, a grizzled middle-aged man with a permanent frown, was dismissing the choirboys. 'I've had to deal with some dim-witted louts in my time,' he was saying in his gentle, cultured voice, 'but none as unmusical and utterly stupid as you lot. For goodness' sake get out of my sight.'

The unmusical, utterly stupid choirboys filed out happily. They thought the world of their choir-master and would have been seriously concerned if he hadn't grossly insulted them at least a dozen times during a practice. The choirmaster's frown turned full on us and he said what a pleasant surprise we were.

'And what about this!' The vicar picked up a large *Ancient and Modern* and battered joyously on the top of the piano. 'I've heard from a curate today. If I can talk him into joining us, we shall be able to open both churches full time. And we shall need them. Mark my words, the by-pass will mean new houses going up all around us – good communications, you see. Such great opportunities! New parishioners, new' – (a really heartwarming thought struck him) – 'new church councillors!'

The choirmaster was carefully peeling some chewing gum off the back of the piano. 'Ah,' he mused. 'I know who did this. I'll slaughter him.'

'And,' finished the vicar triumphantly, 'more boys for your choir.'

'Heaven help us,' said the choirmaster. 'I'll *slaughter* him!'

They don't seem to be building any new houses round the village. The cars are hurtling past it on the six-lane by-pass in ever-mounting numbers and rapidly increasing speeds. Even the one or two that used to find their way through the village street can't bear to leave the by-pass these days.

The vicar is as full of enthusiasm as ever, but he's transferred it to a new thrilling idea. He's going to start a village horticultural society and he's tremendously encouraged by the fact that he's already successfully negotiated with the hardware store for the supply of large quantities of his favourite manure at wholesale prices.

The choirmaster continues to insult grossly precisely the same devoted band of unmusical, stupid choirboys. He is grateful that the age-old revered atmosphere in the choir is not being spoilt by outsiders pushing themselves in. And the congregation are quite happy. They don't like change and decay. They like to know where they are. And they continue to do so – except, of course, when there happens to be a fifth Sunday in the month.

25

Bongo and the Beauty

Few clergymen are called saintly these days. Years ago there were quite a number of saintly clergy around but now the vicar of a village church where Albert, a friend of mine, is in the choir, is probably one of the last of a dying breed. Albert's wife says that goodness shines around the vicar like an unquenchable beacon and he loves everybody and believes that, at bottom, all are saints. He even loves the choir. He says their singing gives a thrilling, spiritual uplift to all who are privileged to hear them Sunday after Sunday.

It is true that most members of the congregation have traditionally put up with the choir stoically enough, even heroically, but never to the extent of regarding them as thrilling, let alone spiritually uplifting. Well, there is just one exception, I suppose – involving the choir's soprano soloist, a quite beautiful girl, known as 'Sweetheart' in the choir, who can bring tears to your eyes singing 'Oh, for the wings of a dove' no matter what kind of disaster the rest of the choir make of the chorus parts. One of the younger churchwardens (nicknamed Bongo after a favourite family dog), the local bachelor Casanova type with a big blatant red sports car and a disturbingly shattering laugh, reckons he's thrillingly, spiritually uplifted every Sunday by just gazing at the beautiful soprano in the choir. His fantasy never gets any further, however, because she's not particularly interested in giving him any spiritual uplift and won't even go to the pictures with him. But, ever confident, he cheerfully perseveres, and supports to the hilt the congregation's revered facade of enthusiastic appreciation of the choir and organist who in turn don't care what the congregation think of them as long as they all turn up at the traditional annual service of thanksgiving for the choir and put a lot of money in the plate for the choir's long established Christmas Dinner at the Fox and Duck. This, according to the vicar's warden, is the dreadful occasion when he, with the vicar, has to endure hours of the kind of singing that is even more coarse and raucous than that at Sunday evensong. However, the warden, a gentle soul who sometimes writes poems on the countryside and peace and tranquility for the local paper, represents the general view of the congregation when he suggests that the feeling about the choir problem should be one of gratitude. After all, he argues, the choir's football riot singing – particularly in the more serene contemplative passages – would be a sight more disorientating were it not for the four-ton Victorian oak memorial choir screen which effectually shields the congregation from the fiercest of the racket.

Anyway, the latest Choir Christmas Dinner Special Service (at which Albert had invited me to help out in the choir) went off without a hitch – at least without any new hitches beyond the regular hitch that it had to take place at all – and everyone went home happy: the choir happy, that the collection was nearly twice as much as last year's; and the congregation happy that the ordeal was over for another twelve months.

We came out of the church into the scented gloaming of a glorious September day. People lingered talking quietly among the ancient tombs and their guardian trees and gently dispersed along the vicarage lane. Here was peace after the turmoil of the choir concert, until turmoil abruptly erupted again in the shape of the blatant red sports car of Sweetheart's admirer that suddenly appeared and screeched to a halt at the lych gate. Bongo sprang out, hailed and beamed at everyone within sight and started polishing the already gleaming chrome parts of the crimson monster. Vigorously he continued to beam and polish until the last few stragglers from the congregation and choir had drifted into the evening shadows and then, doubtless realizing that the source of his thrilling spiritual uplift had once again given him the slip, he drove off to the accompaniment of devilish trumpet strains from the monster's latest horn attachment.

Later, over supper, Albert speculated on the loud young churchwarden's chances of ever improving his prospects with the beautiful soprano. Indeed, the entire congregation and choir have discreetly speculated on the fascinating situation for two or three years now, especially on Sundays in the churchyard as an alternative to discussing the vicar's regular half-hour matins sermons on loving your neighbours and giving generously to the rising-damp-in-the-Vicarage fund.

'Most of us in the choir don't think he's got a dog's chance,' summed up Albert. 'Well, we hope not. This kind of thing has happened before. We get a really good soprano soloist who can read music and sing and then off she goes and gets married and starts having babies and there we are without a soloist again.'

'But Bongo doesn't look as if he's going to give up,' I said.

'No, far from it,' Albert agreed. 'In fact, we've been hearing rumours lately that he's planning to join the choir.'

'Can he sing,' I asked, 'as well as shout?'

'Oh no, of course not,' confirmed Albert, 'and he can't read music either.'

'Well, those deficiencies would stop him joining a choir,' I argued.

'Not our choir, it wouldn't,' said Albert. 'You can't judge our choir by Sweetheart. She's a one-off. She went to a music academy and won a lot of cups and medals and things but the rest of us haven't got any cups or certificates. When we were choirboys here we had a choirmaster who drummed the hymns and psalms into us by continually thumping them out on the piano and making us sing them over and over again till we knew the tune. Only one or two of us had some piano lessons and I learned to play the mouth organ. That was about it.'

'I think the choir manages very well,' I said.

'Well, we've picked up the tenor and bass parts

over the years, of course,' admitted Albert, 'and the vicar says he's thrilled every time he hears us – mind you, it's his fault when we do get into a bit of a mess sometimes. He can't keep in tune or keep quiet and he bawls so loudly that it's hard for the choir to make any headway at all.'

'He means well,' I said.

Albert sighed. 'There are so *many* vicars who mean well these days,' he bemoaned. 'There are some churches around here where the vicars have meant so well that their choirs have disappeared altogether.'

A loud knocking came at the front door. 'It must be *him*,' said Albert. 'Only the vicar knocks in the middle of supper.'

But it wasn't the vicar. Bongo, the churchwarden, strode into the room all eager smiles and enthusiasm. 'I thought I'd have a word with you, Albert, before approaching the maestro ["All-stops-out-Sid-the-organ-grinder"]. I've decided to join the choir!' He stood back to view fully the expected expressions of surprise and overwhelming joy on our faces. 'What do you think of *that*?'

Albert rallied first. 'Well, now, that *is* an idea,' he enthused. 'Sid will welcome you with open arms – especially if you catch him at the right moment when he's overflowing with Christian joy having just mistakenly played "The War March of the Priests" instead of the Bridal March at a big wedding or deliberately played his favourite tune to "Through the Night of Doubt and Sorrow" instead of the vicar's special request. Yes, you'll get in all right.'

And, of course, All-stops-out-Sid *did* accept the new recruit immediately – that was, immediately the new recruit had stood him a pint in the Fox and Duck before choir practice on Friday night. He was used to welcoming into the choir young men of minute or completely non-existent musical ability, unwittingly lured there by the charms of his soprano soloist. There was nothing that warmed his heart more than the sight of the choirstalls crammed to capacity Sunday by Sunday, never mind whether the crammers had the faintest idea about singing. As we assembled, Sid briefly introduced Bongo and directed him to take his place in the back row next to a venerable tenor gentleman who generally spent whole choir practices fiddling with his deaf aid and complaining either that there was no need for Sid to *shout* at the choir or that Sid was deliberately mumbling.

As was his wont, Sid took the practice at breakneck speed, running through half a dozen anthems which the choir knew well and had sung in exactly the same manner for years and years, and devoting the rest of the time to galloping the choir through Sunday's psalms and hymns interspersed with his regular and completely unheeded threats to the boys about what would happen to them if they persisted in turning up late for services, turning the churchyard into a battleground and chewing all through the service. As the practice ended the gentleman with the troublesome hearing aid asked Bongo whether he was tenor or bass, to which Bongo replied that he generally had a go at both depending on how he felt . . .

Sid, being a particularly easy-going, particularly easily satisfied, choirmaster, overlooks almost any musical shortcomings of his singers. That's why he has such a big happy choir (despite the aforementioned tenor gentleman) and singers stay for so long.

Yet there *are* limits, and within weeks of joining the choir Bongo's stentorian vocal efforts had reached and far exceeded them all so that Sid was reluctantly obliged to say and do something to curb that devastating enthusiasm. But even on occasions when a choir member does get too excruciatingly sharp or flat or sings an entirely wrong tune during a service, Sid always discreetly avoids addressing the offender directly, carefully prefacing his criticism with 'There are those among us . . .'

Thus he acted in Bongo's case. Bongo listened intently to Sid's vague words and loyally backed him declaring that he too had been very much aware of the volume of disruptive sounds from the choir which made it difficult for him to sing properly. 'Surely people can *hear* when they are making an almighty hash of things!' he exclaimed later to Sweetheart who he had at last successfully waylaid in the vicarage lane with his roaring red car. 'Surely people can *tell* when they're getting it wrong.'

'You would think so,' agreed Sweetheart.

'And what about me giving you a lift home?' beamed Bongo, opening the car door.

The story goes that, for the first time, Sweetheart actually did accept a lift – and used the opportunity to talk on choir matters. When you really looked into the singing situation at the church, she argued, wasn't it obvious that it was the congregation who were at the heart of the trouble with their football-riot insensitive bawling of the hymns, their plodding along or galloping at half a dozen different speeds that, time after time, simply crippled the choir's professional musicianship?

Bongo was ecstatic, how right, how absolutely right she was. Sweetheart's beautiful hazel eyes held his and brought paradise closer as she mesmerized her delighted victim. And he was the one who could solve the problem, she averred. Only since he had joined the choir had he revealed what a splendid, powerful singing voice he possessed, a voice that could lead and control and uplift – exactly the voice that was so sorely needed down in the congregation to control the whole sorry shambles and produce a united body of praise! His place was down there taking charge of the congregation. The choir, par-

211

ticularly Sweetheart, would be very, very grateful to him.

So Bongo is happily, importantly back in his rightful place in the congregation these days. No one there complains of the extra noise. They all go on as ever, roaring out the hymns they do know and glancing dismissively at the hymns they don't. All is how they like it. All is well. And the saintly vicar continues to love them all – even the choir.

Lightning Source UK Ltd.
Milton Keynes UK
UKHW011830070119
335148UK00009B/573/P

9 781853 114328